Letters in Primitive Christianity

Letters in Primitive Christianity

by
William G. Doty

Fortress Press
Philadelphia

Library of Congress Catalog Card Number 72-87058

ISBN 0-8006-0170-X

Second printing 1977

6583E77   Printed in U.S.A.   1-170

Editor's Foreword

The present volume extends the purpose of this series to deal primarily with the formal, as distinguished from the theological, aspects of the New Testament. This does not mean that the theological has been—or could be—entirely left aside. For one thing that New Testament interpretation has recently been learning from "secular" literary criticism is that form and content in varying degrees—depending on the type or genre of literature—are inseparable; form, as well as content, contributes to meaning. But things which are inseparable in life as lived and understood are often distinguishable for the purposes of analysis, and analysis in turn may contribute to the level of lived understanding. Thus we are concerned to analyze the formal aspects of the New Testament.

The formal qualities of the New Testament's narrative literature have received considerable attention as of late, but relatively few works—though some important ones—have been devoted to the form of the New Testament letter, at least in comparison with the large number of books and articles which continues to deal with Pauline thought and its historical connections. Moreover, the first three volumes of this series have dealt primarily with the Synoptic Gospels and two other New Testament writings, but not with the letters, Pauline or otherwise. It seems, therefore, very appropriate to offer a comprehensive, if not terribly lengthy, account of the form of the early Christian letter, among whose authors Paul is surely the most important.

It may well be that Paul considered a letter to be a fairly poor substitute for his personal presence and the spoken word (see Robert W. Funk, *Language, Hermeneutic, and Word of God* [New York: Harper & Row, 1969]; see also his essay, "The Apostolic *Parousia*: Form and Significance," in *Christian History and Interpretation: Studies Presented to John Knox*, ed. W. R. Farmer, C. F. D. Moule, and R. R. Niebuhr [Cambridge: The University Press,

1967]). There may be, nevertheless, at least one case in which a letter proved to be more effective than his personal presence. I am thinking about Paul's dramatic and fiery relationship with the church at Corinth. At the height of his tensions with that church Paul paid the church a visit and then wrote a letter, a letter which finally brought the church around to repentance and reconciliation. Now perhaps things at Corinth were not really as bad in the first place as Paul thought they were (see Walter Schmithals, *Gnosticism in Corinth: An Investigation of the Letters to the Corinthians,* trans. John E. Steely [New York & Nashville: Abingdon Press, 1971]), in which case Paul's letter would not have accomplished as much as it seems to have or as he possibly thought it had. However, it still remains true that the sharp and anguished letter brought about a result which the painful visit had failed to achieve.

Whether or not the letter—and especially the Pauline letter—is the most effective and viable type of writing in the New Testament is a question which we will continue to debate. But it cannot be denied that these linguistic phenomena have had a long history of provocativeness; thus, we may fruitfully consider how their style and their way of informing their content have helped to bestow upon them their power to be effective.

DAN O. VIA, JR.
University of Virginia

Contents

Preface

Up to the present time epistolary research has remained scattered and fragmentary. There are few if any comprehensive treatments of the epistle in English, and to my knowledge there is no small but inclusive presentation of the epistolary literature of late Hellenism and primitive Christianity such as I have attempted here. At the same time, a survey of the status quo needs to be supplemented by introducing some of the issues now under debate. At several points, then, I have indicated what is more my own private interpretation than the status quo opinion, as when I suggest that Paul's letters represent only a part of the total Pauline epistolary situation.

The book falls into four parts: in the first chapter I have emphasized materials from Graeco-Roman culture which belong to the literary history of primitive Christian literature. We ought to have some idea of the types of letters which the Christians might have used. Chapter two focuses on Paul as the pace-setting epistolographer for all of early Christianity; Paul's letters were carefully composed attempts to continue the guidance of religious communities in which he had a special stake.

Other New Testament epistles are discussed in chapter three, with the emphasis there on the ways in which the various formal subunits of epistolary literature function. There and in chapter four our attention must be on the ways in which an epistolary literature developed in the early church, especially as the letter form was so widely used, and as it was used in contrast to other literary types such as the gospel, history writing, and the apocalypse. This cannot be a major treatise on the development of the letter, nor on world-historical epistolary developments.

Our choice of the particular literary type, the epistle, as the main focus of such a study, reflects the contemporary understanding of the vital importance of comprehending the influence of literary modes, forms, and styles, in the expression of a people's religion. There must be something to the fact that Paul wrote letters, while the memories about Jesus were mostly shared in gospels. Approaching a literary mode historically and structurally, formally rather than by discussion of theology or content, implies that one of the fundamental insights of the discipline of form criticism is being applied: our comprehension and appreciation of a work are vastly increased when our literary expectations are adequately instructed. In other words, what we understand will depend to a large extent on what we expect to understand, or what materials we have come to think of as appropriate for a particular manner of communicating. As one of the first form critics put it, he who begins the analysis of a literary text without an understanding of its form is like a carpenter who begins the building of a house with the roof (paraphrasing Gunkel).

Although we shall see that in Hellenism almost anything could be expressed in epistolary form, the range of material conveyed in primitive Christian letters is fairly circumscribed. In approaching the form, structure, and literary characteristics, we gain a sense of the relative potential for our own lives which these letters may have: we learn what to expect from them, and which questions that might be asked of these letters are appropriate and which inappropriate.

The Society of Biblical Literature now has an ongoing Seminar on the Form and Function of the Pauline Letters, and this Seminar has Task Force groups working on specific phases of the total project. Since completing my Drew University dissertation in 1966 ("The Epistle in Late Hellenism and Early Christianity: Developments, Influences, and Literary Form")—from which some of the substance of this book is taken—I have been encouraged to see quite an expansion of scholarly interest in epistolary studies. Detailed knowledge of epistolary conventions and of the use of the letter in the Hellenistic world should grow considerably as biblical scholars and historians focus upon the literary types (genres) of primitive Christian literature.

I would especially like to acknowledge work in this area by M. Luther Stirewalt, Jr., who has shared many pages of unpublished materials. I would also like to thank those men who criticized and contributed directly to my dissertation research: Karlfried Froehlich, Robert W. Funk, Howard C. Kee, Robert A. Kraft, and David L.

Miller. The Society for Religion in Higher Education awarded me a Post-Doctoral Fellowship for Cross-Disciplinary Study for 1971–72, and I am grateful for this opportunity to study contemporary literary criticism.

Citations of letters are from standard editions for classical writers, and of papyri, from the classification numbers in the main collections (for example, in chapter one, n. 2, "P. BGU #37" refers to papyrus manuscript #37 in the collection, *Berliner Griechische Urkunden*).

I

Epistolary Literature in Hellenism

Communication in letter form may be almost as old as writing. It is a literary form which reaches back into antiquity, probably having developed out of the convention of notching a messenger's staff to remind him of items to be communicated. The development of the letter in antiquity throughout the Ancient Near East is too extensive a topic for discussion here; our period of primary concern begins with the Hellenistic empire, especially since it was under that empire's founder, Alexander the Great (fourth century B.C.E.), that epistolary communication reached a high point of development.

Alexander's administration was wide-reaching and ties between distant geographical parts of the empire were maintained by semi-professional letter writers. The increased emphasis on schooling and the expansion in trade and travel created a ready context for increased letter writing, and Hellenistic rhetoricians and literary critics began to address themselves to the form. (We will discuss some of the theorists and the letter handbooks below; see pp. 8–11.)

Roman letters were even more numerous than Greek-Hellenistic letters; especially around the imperial courts, extensive correspondence was the vogue, and became an important part of courtly training and activity. Some letters were little more than "command performances" at the Caesar's behest—open letters spreading imperial propaganda, such as those of Sallust (86–34 B.C.E.). As public communications, such letters spread official gossip and news of politics and finance, and they were important means of communicating the flavor of life around the Forum throughout the Roman Empire.

The publication of 931 letters by Cicero (106–43 B.C.E.), mostly after Cicero's death, was an event of some importance for the history of the letter, since until their appearance as a collection, no Greek or Roman had dreamed of winning by his letters the approval of educated men. The Roman gentleman had piously saved letters in their rolled form (*capsae*) in his reception room (*tablinum*), more or less the way expensive collections of bound volumes may decorate modern living rooms. But the Ciceronian letters bore a private intensity that had not been found previously—we learn of Cicero's many political intrigues, follow his sponsorship of lower-placed friends, and gain an understanding of his incredible diplomatic verve.

It is not always clear that Cicero was entirely unaware of the possibility that his letters would be published for political purposes; to Trebonius he noted: "You see, I have one way of writing what I think will be read by those only to whom I address my letter, and another way of writing what I think will be read by many" (Ad fam. XV.21.4); and in a letter to Atticus we have an even clearer implication that certain letters might contain the real Cicero, others the public Cicero: "My letters to *you* being of the kind they generally are, I do not like giving them to anybody unless I can be sure that he will deliver them to you" (Ad Att. IV.15.4).

Cicero's political involvements led him to guard against writing anything that might be intercepted and used against him; but in general the tendency in the empire was toward vagueness and superficiality in correspondence, largely due to the haphazard nature of the postal system. More and more the real contents of the messages might be entrusted to a messenger; especially on a delicate matter, the correspondents would have to be linked by a messenger who was trusted by both of them, as demonstrated in a letter of Synesius to Theotimus (#53, about 400 C.E.):

A lengthy letter shows that it is put into the hand of a carrier who is not an intimate of the writer [and hence the letter will not have to do with important details]; but the excellent Acacius [the carrier of this letter] knows my whole mind. He will tell you even more than I have directed him to tell you, for he loves me greatly.[1]

That Cicero did have in mind a selection of his letters (probably only the open, public, and hence rhetorically and rhythmically pol-

---

1. See Johannes Sykutris, "Epistolographie," *Real-Encyclopädie der classischen Altertumswissenschaft,* Suppl. vol. 5 (1931), pp. 199–200.

ished letters) is seen from his letter to Atticus where he states: "There is no collection of my letters, but Tiro has about seventy, and some can be gotten from you. Those I ought to see and correct, and then they may be published" (Ad Att. XVI.5). Cicero's intention to have his letters published surfaced also in a letter a year later to Tiro, where Cicero referred to Tiro's intention to publish: "I see what you are up to; you want your letters also to be put into book form" (Ad fam. XVI.17.1).

Regardless of Cicero's intentions, his collected letters established a pattern that was to remain popular for a long time. Soon letters of the empire were written as much for public consumption as for conveying direct information to individuals. And along with this development went increasing use of the letter form for philosophical and moral exhortation, a tradition which can be found earlier in letters (some genuine) of Plato and Isocrates, Aristotle, Demosthenes, and Epicurus. Horace wrote poetically formed epistles dealing with historical, legal, and grammatical topics; Seneca, Pliny, and Quintillian wrote brief treatises with epistolary features.

Somewhat more akin to some primitive Christian writings are the letters of Apollonius of Tyana (born 4 B.C.E.). Most of them are thought to be spurious, but they illustrate the sort of continuation of religio-philosophical teaching carried on and elaborated by Apollonius's disciples.

Of equal weight with the letters discussed so far—which were transmitted to us in literary sources—are the thousands of personal, private, and business letters in papyri. The importance of these letters has been realized only in this century—most of them have been published only since the 1880s—and specialists in epistolary research are still attempting to integrate what they illustrate about epistolary history and theory. These writings are available to us mostly by chance—they are the remains of official depositories of records, old libraries, dump heaps, and domestic ruins.

The papyrus letters give us a thorough cross section of ancient Hellenistic life, including contracts, business arrangements, family affairs, and communications between friends and acquaintances. While many of these letters were written by scribes, who received training in the proper ways to compose letters, the papyrus letters mostly originated in and reflect the concerns of the lower societal strata, rather than upper class society as reflected in the literary letters.

Similar in type, but generally briefer, are the items written on bits of broken pottery, ostraca. There is no telling how much valuable

3

information was lost in the early phases of archaeological research before the importance of the ostraca was realized. A pre-pulp-paper world seized upon any surplus smooth surface as a medium for writing; for example, pieces of a broken jar or pot might be used for receipts, short business contracts and orders, personal greetings accompanying gifts, and many other purposes. The texts on ostraca are distinguished by their reduction of the message to an unpolished minimum, although they demonstrate the same sense of compulsory use of standard epistolary form found in papyri and in literary letters.

TYPES OF LETTERS

At a later point it will be necessary to distinguish between types of letters when treating the literary history of the letter form vis-à-vis the primitive Christian letters. At this point, however, it will be helpful to have a typical common letter before us in order to have a sense of what is meant by the ordinary primarily private Hellenistic letter:

Mystarion to his own Stotoetis, many greetings! I have sent you my Blastus to get forked sticks for my olive gardens. See that he does not loiter; for you know how I need him every single hour. Farewell. 13 September 50 c.e.[2]

This simple note sent along with a worker is hardly a model of epistolary grace. It is, however, a fairly clear example of a personal business letter, containing the basic formal structure which most Greek letters bore for several centuries: names of writer and addressee, salutation (here in a fairly late, amplified form), body, greeting, plus, in this example, an exact date; the letter does not include the usual phrases of concern for the addressee's health or other formulae. Although this brief sample lacks any particular charm, it is further typical in terms of reflecting simple grammar, brevity, and the epistolary situation—one writer communicating information to another person. And finally Mystarion's note typifies Hellenistic correspondence by its lack of the "personal" traits which we have come to expect in letters. There is little indeed in the Hellenistic letters which reflects the sort of intensely subjective, personalistic, concerns which we anticipate in correspondence. There is no chattiness; there is frequently only the barest mention of the

2. P. BGU #37; reprinted with photographs in Adolf Deissmann, *Light from the Ancient East*, trans. L. R. M. Strachan, 2nd ed. (London: Hodder and Stoughton, 1911), pp. 156 ff.

sender's own immediate situation (beyond stylized references to good or bad health), and wishes and desires are couched in formalized and stylized phrases.

Instead of personal details (letters sent home by travelers do not even mention what they have seen in foreign lands), we are confronted time and time again with a limited variety of stock phrases and a very definite letter form. The form "John to Peter, Greetings," for instance, remained in use from the end of the fourth century B.C.E. until well into the fourth century C.E.[3]

Similar formality, brevity, lack of personal expressions, and stereotyped expression are found in a second example:[4]

Irenaeus to Apollinarius his dearest brother many greetings. I pray continually for your health, and I myself am well. I wish you to know that I reached land on the 6th of the month Epeiph and we unloaded our cargo on the 18th of the same month. I went up to Rome on the 25th of the same month and the place welcomed us as the god willed, and we are daily expecting our discharge, it so being that up till to-day nobody in the corn fleet has been released. Many salutations to your wife and to Serenus and to all who love you, each by name. Goodbye. Mesore 9. (BGU #27, 2nd cent. C.E.)

In these letters we touch upon the formality of the Hellenistic letter tradition, an aspect which will be mentioned again later, especially in conjunction with the Pauline letter form. Before discussing the bases of this formality in Hellenistic letter handbooks and in theoretical remarks about letters, we need to have before us a brief survey of the range of epistolary types which the handbooks treat and which are found in the literary remains of Hellenism. In many cases these types are of little direct relevance to the study of primitive Christian letters, since they are representative of more commercially and politically oriented situations than those found in the earliest Christian letters. Precisely for contrast and context, however, they are worth our attention.

The Business Letter. As in contemporary commerce, a large part of business communication was carried on in Hellenistic times by means of letters. The form was so impelling that hundreds of contracts, surveys, even wills and testaments, were composed in letter form. No little care was given these letters, and scribes were trained in writing appropriate letters for specific situations.

3. See especially Francis X. J. Exler, "The Form of the Ancient Greek Letter" (Diss., Catholic University of America, 1923) and Otto Roller, *Das Formular der Paulinischen Briefe* (Stuttgart: W. Kohlhammer, 1933), p. 418.
4. See also pp. 10 f. and 13.

The Official Letter. Hellenistic political expansion led to increasing need for communication, much of which took place in epistolary form. A number of letters from Hellenistic rulers is extant; juristic decisions were often conveyed in letter form; and military communications form a large part of this type of correspondence. The official letter was of great significance, carrying as it did the sense of the presence of the ruler in epistolary form, and being often intended to establish a new situation or at least to convey directions or information to a large body of persons at once. In addition to readings in the administrative centers, some official letters were posted for public perusal. It may be helpful to compare the epistolary situations of such letters with the primitive Christian epistolary situations, in which one strong leader sent information, directions, and the like, to the Christian communities, as one having the power and authority to do so.

The Public Letter. The letters of Isocrates (436–338 B.C.E.) may have been the first open letters seeking to influence public opinion. Convinced that a strong leader should draw together the discordant Greek states, Isocrates directed four letters to kings extolling national unity. Plato also wrote letters intended as public pleas, as did Speusippos and Alexander. However, such open letters were most frequent during Roman Hellenism, especially during periods of civil strife (Caesar, Antonius, Sallust).

Formal letters of apology and attempts at persuasion also took epistolary form. Common to this type of letter is the suggestion of intimacy with the addressee which was intended to lend credence to the writer's pleas. It might be possible to trace a line of development from such letters, copies of which were surely "leaked" to a number of readers, to the "letters to the editor" columns of our newspapers.

The Non-Real Letter. The term is inept, but it is difficult to find a phrase which will include various letter types such as the pseudonymous letter (written under a name other than that of the actual writer), letters purporting to have come from heaven, and even the epistolary novel. Perhaps "fictitious letters" would do, but that phrase casts aspersions not implied by the original letters.

This type is especially important in the period of our study since it was the period from the fourth century B.C.E. to the third century C.E. that saw the creation of pseudonymous collections by the sophists and others. Part of the exercises in style in Athenian rhetorical schools and in the schools of the empire consisted in writing letters imitating the style of literary or rhetorical masters. Some collections came about almost certainly as the results of school assignments to compose letters in the style of a particular historical figure. The twenty-four letters of Hippocrates, to take one example, were composed by the Hippocratic school as late as 50 C.E. and make up a sort of biographical novel of Hippocrates' life.

There is operative here a notion of literary authorship that is foreign to us, but is reflected time and time again in Hellenistic writing: the pseudonymous or fictitious letter or speech was not thought of as a "forgery" or falsification so much as an expression of how the original figure might have spoken or written. The late Hellenistic and early Roman collections of letters created in the style or spirit of famous personalities of antiquity are therefore to be explained only partially as the result of profit-seeking motives on the part of professional scholars, scribes, and booksellers; they are also responses to public curiosity, attempts to meet apologetic needs, or to supply biographical or edifying information. Such works were considered legitimate extensions of the original writer's own works.

The conception of literature as something to be listened to rather than read silently in private also makes for different ideas of literary property and copyright restriction than those to which we are accustomed. Throughout antiquity even private reading was done aloud—Augustine found it strange that Ambrose read in such a way that his "eyes glanced over the pages" while "his voice and tongue were silent" (*Confessions* 6.3).

Other non-real types include the development of letters in what came to be the novel—we see the beginnings in Alciphron's letters of an Aelian farmer and in Philostratus's erotic letters. Heavenly letters or miraculous letters occur already in the Egyptian Book of the Dead (1500 B.C.E.); in the Hellenistic world Pausanias described a letter by Asclepius which healed the sick when its writing was read out. Finally we may mention magical letters in which someone is contumaciously given over to the dark gods for destruction.

The Discursive Letter. The letter type farthest from the private intimate letter is the discursive letter, which is the nearest epistolary form to the essay. We may distinguish a number of essaylike writings in letter form: alchemical and astrological materials, scientific communications, and paraenetic-didactic letters, with their advice on "how to live" (the classical example came to be Seneca's Letters to Lucilius).

The term preferred for identification of this type by M. Luther

7

Stirewalt is the "letter-essay," a term which avoids the awkward "literary epistle" that is commonly used. Stirewalt discusses such materials from Epicurus, Dionysius of Halicarnassus, Plutarch, and 2 Maccabees and The Martyrdom of Polycarp; he suggests that the letter-essay was a transitional subgenre between personal and official letters and the monograph. Such letter-essays have pronounced epistolary features, especially in openings and closings, and follow epistolary restrictions as to range and style—usually one main topic —and the presentation is in fairly simple diction. Stirewalt has shown that these writings arose primarily in dependence on other, more literary works by the same authors, and that they are intended to supplement or to epitomize the earlier writing, to substitute a later interpretation, or to sketch a future piece of work.[5]

LETTER THEORISTS AND HANDBOOKS

A number of writers expressed opinions about various phases of letter writing. One of the earliest, Artemon,[6] supposedly edited Aristotle's letters and in the process added notes on letter writing which the later Demetrius quoted. "Artemon," according to Demetrius, "says that a letter ought to be written in the same manner as a dialogue, a letter being regarded by him as one of the two sides of a dialogue." A number of later rhetorical writers expressed opinions about letter writing (Dionysius of Alexandria, Apollonius Dyskolus, Theon of Alexandria, commentators on Aristotle), but the work *Peri hermeneias* (*On Style*) by Demetrius, is the most important and the most extensive.

Demetrius's remarks about letter writing come at the end of his section on the "plain" style in rhetoric: he stated that the letter should be in character with the author rather than artificial. It should not be too long, nor should one include frequent breaks in sentence structure, imitating conversation. In disagreement with Artemon, Demetrius felt that a letter should be written more care-

---

5. M. Luther Stirewalt, Jr., "The Form and Function of the Greek Letter-Essay" (photocopy distributed to the Society of Biblical Literature Seminar on the Form and Function of the Pauline Letters, 1971). My category includes letter materials which Stirewalt would exclude by his definition.

6. Either Artemon from Cassandreia, not later than second century B.C.E. (so Sykutris and *Oxford Classical Dictionary*), or the student of Aristotle contemporary with Theophrastus, late fourth century (so Koskenniemi); quotations are from Rudolph Hercher, *Epistolographi Graeci* (Paris: Didot, n.d.—1873?) and T. A. Moxon, ed., Aristotle, *Poetics* and Demetrius, *On Style* (London: J. M. Dent & Sons, Ltd., 1943). Note: Numbers in the text after Demetrius's quotes refer to paragraphs in *On Style*.

fully than a dialogue since it forms a sort of literary present to its recipient, and "a picture of his [the writer's] own soul" (#227). Plato and Thucydides are criticized for writing letters in stilted language that are only treatises with letter headings. A certain freedom should prevail over the more calculated writing that lacks the friendship essential to letters, and which "calls a fig a fig" (#229). There are epistolary topics just as there is an epistolary style; logical subtleties and natural history should be excluded. Use of proverbs and old sayings may augment the finesse required to express one's affections and friendship, but a writer should not play the artificial role of a sycophant. A letter should be an expression of one's friendly feelings (*philophronesis*) in brief compass, an expression of a simple subject in simple terms.

Several important aspects of the Greek letter tradition are evident in Demetrius's treatment: (a) Demetrius was setting forth rules for letter writing based on the authority of past masters. He especially appeals to Aristotle, "who is thought to have been exceptionally successful in attaining to the epistolary manner" (#230). (b) But in Demetrius's day letters were somewhat different; they were still related to dialogue, but not so closely related as to permit the stylistic devices of the literary dialogue (oratorical display, periods and imitative speech, elevated mannerisms) or the scientific discursiveness of the treatise. (c) If the letter was related to dialogue—or to conversation—its primary place in human intercourse was as an expression of friendship. Such friendly relationship was to be expressed in the letter with more freedom than in the literary dialogue, and without formal periods of rhetoric. (d) Ornamentation was not to be excluded, even though the letter should be in the plain rather than the elevated style, but it ought to be restricted to the sort of everyday material appropriate to friendship and not given to moralistic pronouncements. The honesty appropriate to the trust of friendship should displace labored circumlocutions or artificial conventions.

In many ways the statements of Demetrius summarize the theory of letter writing in Greek and Roman literary circles that prevailed for several centuries; in subsequent theoretical remarks by Theon, Cicero, Quintillian, and Gregory of Nazianzus, the main points we have enumerated appear again and again. In both practice and theory, letter writing remained conservative and stable.

What appear to be desk guides for letter writing, letter handbooks, have been transmitted, one in the name of Demetrius and one in the name of Proclus or Libanius. These handbooks gave

9

practical introduction to avoiding troublesome errors, as well as basic patterns for certain types of letters. They analyzed how certain letters ought to be written, quoting examples to demonstrate how particular nuances ought to be conveyed. Among the letter types discussed are letters of friendship, introduction, blame, reproach, consolation, criticism, censure, praise, interrogation, accusation, apology, and gratitude—in all, some twenty-one types in Demetrius's *Tupoi epistolikoi* (*Epistolary Types*), and forty-one in Proclus's *Peri epistolimaiou charakteros* (*Concerning the Epistolary Type*). Additional handbooks and school copybooks appear in the papyri, giving evidence of training in letter composition as an aspect of training in the schools.[7]

On the basis of the few pure examples of the handbook types found in the papyri, it seems that the guides were not very influential. It is only the letter of introduction or commendation (*epistole sustatike*) that is found to any extent. The following quotations illustrate what Demetrius and Proclus have to say about this type of letter, together with two additional examples, one the attached note in Romans 16:1–2 and the other an example from the papyri:

Demetrius: The introductory type, which we write to someone on behalf of another, including praise while making acquainted those who were unacquainted. An example: XX, who is conveying this letter to you, is a man we have proven and whom we love because of his faithfulness. Please be hospitable to him both for my sake and his, and indeed for your own sake also! You will not be at all sorry if you trust him with either words or deeds of a confidential sort in whatever you wish. When you have learned how useful he can be in everything, you will even praise him yourself to others.

Proclus: It is by an introductory letter that we introduce a person to someone else (it is also called the letter of recommendation). The letter: This honorable and sought-after man whom you receive should be treated hospitably, for I have been grateful to him on account of his distinguished dealing in my behalf.

Paul: I introduce to you our sister Phoebe, who is a deaconess of the church which is at Cenchrea, in order that you may receive her in the Lord in a way worthy of the saints and that you may help her in anything she may have need of you; for she has herself been a helper of many and indeed of myself as well.

P. Oxy. 746: Theon to Heraclides his brother, many greetings and wishes for good health. Hermophilus the bearer of this letter is [the friend or

7. Sykutris, "Epistolographie," p. 198; Deissmann, *Light from the Ancient East,* p. 222, nn. 1 and 2; see Heikki Koskenniemi, *Studien zur Idee und Phraseologie des griechischen Briefes bis 400 n. Chr.* (Helsinki: Suomalaien Tiedeakatemie, 1956), pp. 57–59.

relative] of —erius, and asked me to write to you. Herophilus declares that he has business at Kerkemonus. Please therefore further him in this matter as it is just. For the rest take care of yourself that you may remain in good health. Goodbye.

Other letter types are sparsely represented, but all in all the guide-books do not seem to have had much direct influence. Even though they may not have been followed word-for-word, however, any more than contemporary handbooks, they indicate that letter *theorists* were very much aware of the range of letter types. If the handbooks are particularly "vulgar" and intended for quick reference, still the general framework of daily practice was established by the schools and by letter theorists. (A comparison between homiletic guides and actual sermons would probably disclose that the same relationship exists between them as between handbooks and actual letters.)

CHARACTERISTIC FEATURES OF THE GREEK LETTER

The most extensive study of the Greek letter which attempts to relate such matters as letter handbooks to letter theorists and to the actual practice of letter writing in the papyri is the Oslo dissertation by Heikki Koskenniemi to which reference has already been made (the title in English would read: Studies in the Concept and Phraseology of the Greek Letter to 400 C.E.). Koskenniemi abstracts three general characteristics of the Greek letter which he takes to be crucial to understanding the uniqueness, purpose, and function of the Greek letter.

The first aspect, and the most important one, is what Koskenniemi identifies as *philophronesis*, that is, that the letter served the purpose of expressing "the friendly relationship" between two persons. On the basis of this implied standard, theorists often rejected as out of place materials of a technical or scientific nature. Letter style and phraseology were to express in writing the friendly intercourse that excluded artificial affectation; as a sort of written gift of oneself (Demetrius), Hellenistic letters were to reflect the giving of oneself found in oral meetings.

In light of the extreme stereotyping found in Hellenistic letters, which will be discussed next, and the accompanying sense of impersonality—at least according to our tastes—it is at first striking that Koskenniemi identifies the "philophronetic" element as having been given primary importance. He demonstrates convincingly from ref-

11

erences to the epistolary situation itself, however, that the forms and structures to which Greek letters were so strongly bound were at least linguistically rooted in the friendship relationship. Even such expressions as "dearest," or "most honorable" (*philtatos, timiotatos and glukutatos*), or "my own" (*idios*—often for slaves!) are basically intended to reflect the meeting of the correspondents face to face.[8]

The second aspect, *parousia* or "presence," Koskenniemi takes to express the special purpose of writing: a letter was intended to revive the existence of a friendship when the correspondents were physically separated. So for instance Proclus (#2) mentioned that a letter writer should write "to someone not present as if he were present." The sense in which Paul reflects on the possibility of his future presence with correspondents (the "apostolic parousia" and travelogue) will be discussed in chapter two.

To designate the main function of the letter, the continuance of a dialogic conversation in writing, Koskenniemi chooses the term *omilia*, "homily," a term used along with *dialogos*, "dialogue," in later Hellenistic texts to describe the tone of epistolary discourse.[9] (Both terms later acquired specific rhetorical meanings which were similar to contemporary usage: homily—sermon, dialogue—treatise with two speakers or points of view.)

Koskenniemi has done us a service in identifying these three essential aspects of the Greek letter, thus bringing into prominence the features which an educated Greek might have listed as characteristic of the nature of the letter. In addition to these three characteristics there are other features which are striking when one reads many Hellenistic letters—features that are not so much philosophical as practical.

Probably the most striking feature to someone who has read through Hellenistic letters in Greek and in Latin from about the fourth century B.C.E. to the fourth century C.E., is the fact that they are so amazingly stereotyped and bound to tradition. Especially phrases of concern for the other's health, greetings, and mention of thinking about the other person or praying for him, appear again and again, in phrases which change so slowly that the history of

8. Koskenniemi argues that this emphasis on friendship reflects the influence of Aristotelian theory about the nature of community, and gives references to the *Nichomachean Ethics* on p. 37, nn. 2 and 3.

9. This is the sense of the wording in both Gregory Nazianzus (Epp. 87, 93), and Basil (Epp. 239, 269 and elsewhere).

the letter can actually be charted by these minute and gradual modifications.

The emphasis upon repeating common phrases belonging to letter tradition is probably a characteristic of letter writing in general: compare the way thousands of our letters begin "Dear Sir." But in the Greek letters, especially, which are mostly quite brief, the use of a limited number of stereotyped phrases lends a very impersonal quality to the letters which is less frequent in contemporary correspondence. Even family letters betrayed little emotion according to our sensibilities, and content is restricted to formulaic expressions of good wishes, polite inquiry, or business. Here is a typical example, a letter from Serapion to his brothers concerning his forthcoming marriage:

Serapion to his brothers Ptolemaeus and Apollonius greeting. If you are well, it would be excellent. I myself am well. I have made a contract with the daughter of Hesperus and intend to marry her in the month of Mesore. Please send me half a chous of oil. I have written to you to let you know. Goodbye. Year 28, Epeiph 21. Come for the wedding-day, Apollonius. (P. Par. 43, 154 B.C.E.)

There was a very limited amount of freedom to modify and adapt epistolary conventions—and deviations are mainly restricted to modifications of grammar or use of alternate choices of greetings. The end result is not a canvas of infinite variation and color and technique, but rather a mass-produced print of stereotyped phrases, rigid external structure, of brevity and of a detached impersonality matched only by our own most formal invitations and announcements—or by this letter of 1477 in which Margaret Paston wrote to her husband:

Right reverend and worshipful husband, I recommend me to you, desiring heartily to hear of your welfare, thanking you for the token ye sent me by Edmund Perys, praying you to weet that my mother sent to my father to London for a gown cloth of Mustyrdevyllers to make a gown for me. . . .

Not only standardized formulaic phrases within the letters, but also the overall literary form of the Greek letter remained constant from about the third century before to the third century of the Common Era.[10] This form may be briefly outlined as follows:

10. Exler, "The Form of the Ancient Greek Letter," p. 12; Roller, *Das Formular der Paulinischen Briefe*, pp. 56, 68.

Introduction (prescript or salutation)
    including: sender, addressee, greetings, and often additional
    greetings or wish for good health
Text or Body, introduced with characteristic introductory formulae
Conclusion
    including: greetings, wishes, especially for persons other than
    the addressee; final greeting or prayer sentence; and sometimes
    dating.

Many hundreds or even thousands of private letters, and many
hundreds of more public letters could be listed, having this same
basic formal structure.

Divergences are not rare, but they are mainly divergences in
terms of more flowery language, more extensive expressions of
relationship, or multiplication of addressees or of those indirectly
greeted. These conventions are present even in official letters, although in these the concluding greetings were often omitted or
replaced by attesting signatures, dating, or a note as to where the
original document was recorded. Otherwise the date is missing as
frequently as it is given (year—number of year—month—day);
where it is included, it is usually mentioned because of its special
importance to the recipient, and hence is seldom lacking in official
letters.

If we speak of "the Hellenistic letter form," then, it is with such
a pattern in mind. The sense of pattern was so strong that one of
the traits of Theophrastus's figure Arrogance was that he deviated
from normal letter practice (Characters, #24)!

Among the requirements of epistolary style was the requirement
put forth by Demetrius (#230) that only things having an epistolary character (*epistolika pragmata*) should be discussed. Defin-
ing what such "things" might be, Demetrius noted that Aristotle
had excluded "logical subtleties" and "questions of natural history."
We have already seen that it is difficult to restrict "letter" to a
particular type of letter—that there are various types, and to speak
of "letter theory" can mean several things. Here we need to realize
that Demetrius was referring primarily to the resistance offered by
the theorists to writing treatises in letter form. Hence as far as style
is concerned we can list brevity as the key; Demetrius stated that a
letter ought not to become a treatise with a letter greeting (##228,
231, 234). Brevity was also demanded by the size of a single sheet
of papyrus (which would be rolled and sealed), or by the occasion

14

of having to respond quickly in order that a messenger could carry back an answer.

Clarity was especially required. Philostratus criticized Aspasius for writing obscurely (De vit. soph. 2.33) while Antipater was praised for a clear style (2.24). Language used in letters was supposed to be modeled on the everyday speech of educated men, without slipping into vulgarities. It should occupy a middle place between elevated diction (*logoeides*) and carefree speech (*lalikon*). A total lack of ornamentation suggested cheapness (*euteleia*) and was impolite; too much implied want of taste (*aperokalia*) and was pretentious. Brief quotations or references were not out of place, and proverbs and comic phrases were especially liked in cultured letters; elaborate rhetorical devices, however, were to be excluded.

The sense of restrictiveness in terms of content is almost as great as the sense of pressure to utilize only the one standard form, and we find writers voicing dissatisfaction that letters were so restricted. Pliny, for instance, wrote: "I would have our letters be those which contain something out of the ordinary and sordid and confined to private interests," and asked "Why must our letters always concern such petty domestic items?" (3.20). So too Seneca criticized Cicero for telling Atticus to write just for the sake of writing even it nothing had entered his head: ". . . there will always be something for me to write about, even if I leave out the various types of news with which Cicero fills up his letters . . ." (118.1–2).

SUMMARY: HELLENISTIC LETTERS

1. *Contents.* In Hellenism the epistolary mode became so inclusive that almost any type of material could be presented in letters. At the same time, certain restrictions were made: most theorists assumed that the private letter of friendship was the norm, and felt that the letter should not be a treatise or a dialogue. Used to some extent for communication of scientific knowledge, the letter did not lend itself to formalized presentations, for which the treatise or the literary dialogue was more suited. Ethical and moral questions were discussed in letter form (Epicurus, Seneca), but these "letters" are closer to treatises than to private letters, and should probably be called letter-essays.

The papyrus letters demonstrate a range of subject matter related to details of providing for daily needs and making arrangements of every sort: for bringing along a forgotten cloak, sending a pot of honey or a set of crockery, caring for family left at home, sending stipends to students or salaries to wives, arranging marriages or other contracts, complaining about officials, seeking or giving advice, hiring and firing, introducing and commending.

2. *Purpose.* Communications for political, commercial, or military purposes of the state were conveyed primarily in letter form. So too, the man in the street employed the letter for his day-to-day arrangements. By and large, friendship was maintained by letters, and letter theorists could speak of maintaining friendship as the primary function of the letter.

3. *Development.* Specialized epistolary forms developed, such as the poetic epistle, the letter of introduction, or the letter of consolation. Letter collections began to be made, promoted by the great libraries and the schools. More strictly private letters also grew in volume. Among the Romans an entire etiquette of correspondence developed, and the frequency of letters could constitute a test of friendship (Cicero, Ad fam. II.2.1). It became a matter of politeness to send a letter to a friend whenever possible (Ad Att. VII.1); Caesar, by not replying to a letter from Clodius, expressed his sympathy with Clodius's opponent, Cicero (Ad Quint. frat. III.1.11). The tradition developed to the point that in the fourth century Synesius remarked in a letter to Theotimus: "I send you this letter more for the sake of a customary greeting than because there is need of one."[11]

4. *Context and Situation.* The letter was primarily a means of maintaining contact between two individuals. It could also serve this purpose between a writer and several addressees or between writers and addressees. Although we have relatively few letters with plural addressees, this type of letter is probably the closest analogue between the New Testament epistles and Graeco-Roman Hellenistic epistolography.

The letter is also primarily a function of a previous relationship. Friendship or a familial relationship was presupposed for most private correspondence; a commercial, pedagogical, or military relationship was often the background of the less private letter. The letter came to be understood as the representative of its writer. In a legal decision, the letter represented how a judge would have ruled in person; in a contract, each party was represented as contracting in person. In each case, then, the original situation implied by the language

11. Synesius #53; in Hercher, *Epistolographi Graeci*, p. 662. The statement can also be taken to indicate that the real message was being sent via the carrier rather than in the letter itself.

and by the form of the letter is the personal confrontation, the conversation, or the oral encounter.

The private letter primarily presupposed a reply in deed or by letter. Hired letter writers and carriers often waited for a reply before returning to the original writer. For very casual notes a hinged tablet with soft wax writing surfaces (the diptych) was often used; after rubbing out the original letter, the respondent could enter his reply on the same material.

In less private letters, the impulse to pass on information or advice, often from one in authority, is frequently expressed. Some letters obviously expected future correspondence to include some indication that instructions given had been followed. Less private letters seem to have been written often with the primary intent of producing a written document, rather than leading to a personal response. It is of course a matter of degree, and many quite stilted letters are represented among the most private letters; but the less private letters in general are least dependent upon the orginal relationships of the correspondents. These letters often seem to be independent of any continuance of the relationship, and are one-sided in point of view.

In the more private letters, however, we have to do mainly with conditions in which there is anticipated a continuation, change, or growth of the personal relationship, and/or a reply, either by letter or in person or through fulfillment of some obligation. In the less private letters we have to do with one-directional relationships to a much larger extent, as teacher-to-student. While the differentiation between whether a future of the relationship is expected or not may not be helpful for the purposes of classification (for example an "official letter" might above all others require a response from a lesser official!), the distinction is helpful if we attempt to define or to explore subsequent or contemporaneous examples of the epistolary mode within a specific community.

PRIMITIVE CHRISTIAN LETTERS

Introduction of the various Hellenistic letter types in a book on "primitive Christian letters" might be understood as following the usual rationale that the primitive Christian letters are derivative from those Hellenistic letters. A recent session of the Society of Biblical Literature's Seminar on the Form and Function of the Pauline Letters centered around study of Philemon as a key to the Pauline collection—assuming that Philemon, being the shortest Pauline letter, and seemingly closest in form to Hellenistic traditions, might serve as a paradigm for understanding the other letters. Actually, responses to the main paper suggested that Philemon may function more clearly as the exception to the Pauline letter collection rather than as the norm. Nonetheless, it would be irresponsible to assume that there are no contacts between the Hellenistic traditions and the primitive Christian letters, and until the final verdict is in, scholarship will continue to work with Hellenistic and primitive Christian letters in tandem.

Before focusing on the Pauline collection, we need to have before us a quick overview of the range of use of letters in primitive and early Christianity, anticipating more detailed analysis in chapters three and four.

The earliest Christian letters which concern us are those written by Paul around the middle of the first century. While we may not assume that there were no other letters written before Paul's, or that we possess all the letters Paul wrote, transmitted tradition has been restricted to the canonical Pauline letters as the earliest literary products in primitive Christianity; from time to time we catch glimpses of pre-Pauline traditional materials, and possibly fragments of pre-Pauline letters, but the main focus has to remain centered upon the Pauline letters in the New Testament.

A second group of materials in letter form appeared in sequence with and probably in dependence upon the Pauline letters, namely, those writings in the general style of Paul and in his name, which are variously called the Post-Pauline, Deutero-Pauline, Pseudo-Pauline, or more traditionally, the Pastoral Letters (1 and 2 Timothy, Titus). We argue later that these letters are thought to continue the Pauline letter tradition; from the point of view of their contents, they are written to express what their authors felt Paul would have said in their own later situations if he had remained alive. Some of these materials begin to spring the true-letter framework, tending to become essays or treatises, a tendency especially prominent in a group of writings associated with the name of John, the Johannine Epistles (1, 2, and 3 John). A fourth set of letters can be identified in the second volume of Luke's two-volume account of primitive Christianity, in Acts 15:23–29 and 23:26–30.

A fifth group of letters is associated with the names of prominent leaders: the Universal ("Catholic") Letters, comprised of 1 and 2 Peter, James, and Jude. And finally, within the canon of the New Testament, a group of letters is recorded in the Apocalypse to John

(Rev. 2–3). Arguments concerning the authenticity of all these post-Pauline materials will be considered in chapter four, where later letters are also discussed. Here we need only to indicate that the post-Pauline tradition becomes richer and richer from the standpoint of the use of the epistolary genre. Letters figure as one of the most important literary modes in early Christianity from the third century; a great deal of the theological discussion, administrative communication, and general business of the developing Christian church was carried out through letters.

Twenty of the twenty-seven New Testament writings purport to be letters and we have seen that two of the seven remaining writings, Acts and the Apocalypse to John, contain materials purporting to be letters. Even if we exclude additional materials which are letters in only part of their formal structure—Hebrews, James—it can still be seen that the dominant literary form found within the Christian canon is the letter. And within the next oldest body of Christian literature, the "Apostolic Fathers," the form is still dominant (1 Clement, Ignatius, Polycarp, The Martyrdom of Polycarp). Later Christian writings continue to demonstrate epistolary form to such an extent that a major chronicle of church history and Christian thought could be derived from writings exclusively styled in epistolary form.

II

The Pauline Letters

The Pauline letters have fascinated people for generations. Primarily looked upon as a major Christian theologian, Paul has also been studied as a writer within the context of Hellenistic literature. Our concern must be with Paul the writer rather than with Paul the theologian, although there will be several points at which suggestions about Paul's method of doing theology will arise from observations about his method of writing. In this chapter the stress is upon the ways we may speak of a Pauline form and structure. Since there are differences between the earlier and the later letters, we catch sight of this form and structure as it is taking shape. I argue that Paul was the person who adapted Graeco-Roman letter models for Christian purposes, that in his letters a genre or subgenre was created, and that our task is that of identifying the stages and steps in generic construction. Instead of arguing that there is one clearly identified Pauline form, I argue that there is a basic understanding of structure by which Paul wrote, but that this basic understanding could be modified on occasion, and that the basic understanding itself was something that came into being only gradually. I am not as concerned to argue the case for developmental stages in Pauline thought or literary concept[1] as to convince the reader that when he reads the Pauline correspondence, he is witnessing the creation of a genre which was to have an impressive afterlife. Certain post-Pauline letters revert to more orthodox Hellenistic letter models; others slavishly imitate Paul. But at no time after the writing and publication of the Pauline letters were early Christian writers able to ignore the impact of the Pauline letters. They were the model for early Christian literature in ways that the gospels and histories

1. See John C. Hurd, *The Origins of I Corinthians* (New York: Seabury Press, 1965), Chap. 1, and Victor P. Furnish, "Development in Paul's Thought," *Journal of the American Academy of Religion* 38 (1970): 289–303.

could not be, and the line of generic contact continued from Paul down through the encyclicals and papal letters of subsequent centuries.

ADAPTATIONS AND MODIFICATIONS

Paul seems to have had a sense of freedom in literary matters corresponding to the freedom in theology that many commentators have noted. Instead of remaining tied to literary models, for instance, he combined non-Jewish Hellenistic customs with Hellenistic Jewish customs, and created a form which cannot be equated with either tradition. The most obvious place in the Pauline letters where this fusion can be identified is in the very first part of the typical Pauline letter, in the phrase "Grace to you and peace. . . ." This phrase includes a modification of the stereotyped "greetings!" of Hellenistic letters (*chairein* becomes *charis*, "grace") and the characteristic "peace" (*shalom*) of Jewish letters. (See below, "The Form of the Pauline Letters"; the letters created for Acts do not demonstrate this fusion of terms, but have normal Hellenistic openings.)

Other, more subtle changes have been chronicled by John L. White and others. These changes include: (a) closing: inclusion of a (liturgically-formulated?) benediction, which functions as the Hellenistic farewell; (b) thanksgiving: this signals the reason for writing, and is not thanksgiving for rescue from danger but for the addressee's faithfulness; (c) body: adaptation of formulaic expressions for purposes of Pauline teaching and preaching.[2]

It is difficult if not impossible to establish any direct lines of borrowing by Paul from Jewish epistolary materials in terms of their form and structure. We have already indicated that he evidently appropriated the Shalom greeting, but other than that our sources are too meager to indicate precise parallels. He must have known Jewish correspondence within Israel, since we learn that Jewish officials and missionaries there carried letters of introduction and recommendation (Acts 5:34, 15:22–29, 28:21). We also have evidence of correspondence between rabbinic authorities and communities outside Israel; these letters were of a pastoral type, and are

2. John L. White, "The Structural Analysis of Philemon: A Point of Departure in the Formal Analysis of the Pauline Letter" (photocopy for the Society of Biblical Literature Seminar on the Form and Function of the Pauline Letters, 1971), pp. 27 f., 30–32, 34–45; Jack T. Sanders, "The Transition from Opening Epistolary Thanksgiving to Body in the Pauline Corpus," *Journal of Biblical Literature* (hereinafter cited as *JBL*) 81 (1962): 352–53, 358–62.

the origins of the *responsa* form in Judaism, in which famous or respected rabbinical teachers responded to questions from diaspora Jews.[3] Since the letters referred to in Talmudic sources are associated with the Pharisaic tendency within first-century Judaism, they provide evidence that Pharisaic leaders exerted influence throughout Israel and the diaspora. According to the book of Acts, when Paul arrives in Rome, he is greeted by Jews who state that they are eager to hear his views and that they have not received any letters warning them about his teachings (28:21). The implication is that such letters could have been expected.[4] Jewish epistolary materials primarily reflect official letter traditions rather than personal letter traditions; the possible continuity between Jewish letters and primitive Christian letters is difficult to establish, and seems less important (because of its restricted compass and lack of formal continuity) than the contacts with Hellenistic correspondence.

The other type of Hellenistic letters which might be thought to have influenced Paul in his choice of literary mode would be the correspondence between a teaching master such as Epicurus or Apollonius and his followers. The problem with the Epicurean correspondence is that it has been very heavily edited (redacted) by Epicurus's followers who amplified the master's teachings and adapted them to later situations. Correspondence from Apollonius of Tyana is so mixed with obvious pseudonymous letters that it is almost impossible to reconstruct; letters are addressed to groups of recipients (Lacedaemonians, Ephesians, Milesians, Trallians) as well as to individuals.

The letters just discussed can be included within epistolary classifications only by a good deal of forcing; we should probably accept Stirewalt's designation "letter-essay" for these materials and for the extensive materials of late Hellenism that have traditionally been called "epistles," especially since "literary epistle" remains a technical identification for Latin *epistulae* which are less letters than formal treatises.

The distinction between epistle and letter is a distinction common in many introductions to early Christian literature, having been established in New Testament scholarship toward the end of the

3. References are summarized conveniently in Jacob Neusner, *A Life of Yohanan ben Zakkai. Ca. 1–80 C.E.*, 2nd ed. rev. (Leiden: E. J. Brill, 1970); and in M. Luther Stirewalt, Jr., "A Survey of the Uses of Letter-Writing in Hellenistic and Jewish Communities through the New Testament Period" (photocopy for SBL Seminar, 1971), pp. 31–38.
4. Neusner, *A Life of Yohanan ben Zakkai*, pp. 238 and 41.

23

nineteenth century. In spite of attempts by nineteenth-century philologists and historians of Hellenistic literature to give the New Testament letters the same literary value as classical texts, the primitive Christian literature was more and more treated as "popular" literature, and hence regarded as hardly worth scholarly attention. Toward the end of the century, however, the many papyri began to be discovered and published, and scholars began to explore the similarities between life and letters in the papyri and in the New Testament. It soon began to be evident that the literary family in which the primitive Christian literature was most at home was to be located somewhere in between the classical materials and the papyrus materials with their concern for everyday affairs.

Adolf Deissmann, a pioneer in publishing and studying the papyrus materials, emphasized the close relationships, especially in terminology and references to contemporary life, between primitive Christian and Hellenistic culture represented in the papyri. Happy to see that the Christian literature no longer had to be judged on the basis of classical Hellenistic literature, Deissmann attempted to swing the pendulum over to the other side: he thought that the New Testament letters, especially, were to be studied in conjunction with the life and letters of the papyri, which he took to be substantially more "natural" than the classical writings.

Deissmann suggested that scholarship should differentiate between artistic, artificial materials and natural, daily materials, and so he developed a distinction between "epistles" and "letters." The former category was to include anything written especially for publication or for artistic effect; the latter category included materials in which the "soul life of antiquity" was exposed—materials written not for future artistic or aesthetic appreciation, but purely for the momentary needs of situations. Paul's letters were to be considered "letters" (*Briefe*), not "epistles" (*Episteln*); and by this distinction Deissmann meant to stress the genuine, unaffected religious impulse which the letters disclosed.[5]

For Deissmann, it was extremely important to understand Paul's letters not as theological treatises (along with other early comparative-religions scholars, Deissmann was extremely suspicious of "theology"), but as private letters. Paul's letters should be read as in-

---

5. See Deissmann, *Light from the Ancient East*, pp. 290–302 and 409. I have traced the ways Deissmann's presuppositions influence his conclusions in "The Classification of Epistolary Literature," *Catholic Biblical Quarterly* 31 (1969): 185 ff.

formal private notes, "the outcome of a definite situation, which could not be repeated, and [which referred] only to this particular situation. . . ."[6]

Since Deissmann wrote, New Testament scholars have come to realize that Paul's letters are by no means "private personal letters" in the usual sense of that term. Rather, they were written to communities of Christian believers for use in their common life, and they were written by Paul in his self-conscious capacity as an official representative of early Christianity (as an "apostle"). D. J. Selby points out that:

. . . these letters are not, strictly speaking, private letters. As their character clearly shows they were written to be read before the congregation to which they were addressed. The second personal plural, the allusions to various persons, and the greetings and salutations make them group communications.[7]

References within the Pauline letters provide ample proof that the letters are more than semi-private personal letters:

1 Thess. 5:27, "I adjure you by the Lord that this letter be read to all the brethren."

Philemon v. 2b, ". . . the church in your house. . . ."

2 Thess. 3:14–15, reference to the impact of the letter in the church.

Martin R. P. McGuire reminds us of the importance of remembering that letters in antiquity were read out loud in a low voice:

This practice obviously had great influence on epistolary composition and style. It also helped to make the letter addressed to an individual or a group an easy and natural vehicle for philosophical or religious discussion or exposition.[8]

Far from being casual letters of the type found predominantly in the papyri, Paul's letters were intended for public use within the religious gatherings; each letter "was to be read publicly in the church time and time again in order to teach, to lead, to secure the

6. Adolf Deissmann, *Paul: A Study in Social and Religious History*, trans. W. E. Wilson, 2nd ed. (New York: Harper & Brothers, 1957), p. 12.

7. D. J. Selby, *Toward the Understanding of St. Paul* (Englewood Cliffs: Prentice-Hall, Inc., 1962), p. 239.

8. Martin R. P. McGuire, "Letters and Letter Carriers in Christian Antiquity," *Classical World* 53 (1960): 150.

stance of Christian men."[9] A letter of Dionysius of Corinth to the Romans (ca. 170 C.E.) referred, according to Eusebius, ". . . to Clement's Epistle to the Corinthians, proving that from the very first it had been customary to read it in church":

Today being the Lord's Day, we kept it as a holy day and read your epistle, which we shall read frequently for its valuable advice, like the earlier epistle which Clement wrote on your behalf.[10]

Having overcome Deissmann's restriction of the Pauline letters to private letters, we must not, of course, simply revert to the previous position which treated them as primarily dogmatic essays. Subsequent scholarship has reached something of a balance between treating Paul's letters as purely occasional, contextual writings, directed only to specific situations, and as attempts to express a Christian understanding of life which had ramifications for theological expression beyond the particular historical situation.

Part of the problem in trying to achieve a balanced understanding of the Pauline letters is that the letters have entered the Christian scriptural canon; as Schubert notes, the scholar must now dispose of ". . . the genetically irrelevant form and function which they have assumed and discharged through the centuries as a distinct and distinguished part of the New Testament canon."[11] An approach to the letters such as that pursued here treats the New Testament letters as literary materials from Graeco-Roman Hellenistic religions, not as sacred texts immune to criticism. At the same time critical studies must recognize that certain of the primitive Christian letters were considered especially relevant and important, leading to inclusion in the canon. Paul, insofar as he was not writing as a private person but as an apostle, and not primarily to individual persons but to churches, did indeed write letters which had a public intent, bringing them closer to the official pronouncement than to the private letter. He wrote to instruct, to give advice, to encourage or reprimand; he taught, preached, and exhorted in the letters. But he did not write dogma of the sort represented by the Epicurean let-

9. Adolf von Harnack, *Die Briefsammlung des Apostels Paulus* . . . (Leipzig: Hinrichs, 1926), p. 11.

10. From the early fourth-century work by Eusebius, *The History of the Church from Christ to Constantine* 4.23, trans. G. A. Williamson (Baltimore: Penguin Books, 1965), p. 185.

11. Paul Schubert, "Form and Function of the Pauline Letters," *Journal of Religion* 19 (1939): 367.

ters; he did not step out of the immediate epistolary situation to write treatises with only an epistolary flavoring.

Indeed, Paul wrote in every letter from the point of view of one immediately involved with a specific situation: "Sociologically speaking every letter is the direct result of and a primary factor in a concrete case of social interaction."[12] As suggested above, every letter represents what Paul thought ought to be addressed to the specific situation, and we often have a sense that Paul is preaching as if he were there in person: "It is as a substitute for personal action that he writes his letters."[13]

THE FORM OF THE PAULINE LETTERS

We have seen that the basic form of the Hellenistic letter contains a threefold division: an introductory section, the main body of the letter, and a concluding section. (Indeed I would argue that any communication carries three such features, and that means that the three features must be more clearly subdivided for identification and study.) Paul's letters fit the Hellenistic pattern in most respects, although we shall see that he developed certain subunits and expanded others.

The basic form which we may identify as belonging to the Pauline way of writing letters is as follows:

Opening (sender, addressee, greeting)

Thanksgiving or Blessing (often with intercession and/or eschatological climax)

Body (introductory formulae; often having an eschatological conclusion and/or an indication of future plans)

Paraenesis

Closing (formulaic benedictions and greetings; sometimes mention of the writing process).

The contemporary emphasis on the formal nature of Paul's letters is an important corrective to two older viewpoints: the first, represented by Friedrich Köster, suggested that Paul's material was

---

12. Schubert, "Form and Function of the Pauline Letters," p. 376.
13. Von Williamowitz, quoted by Johannes Weiss, *Earliest Christianity,* ed. F. C. Grant (New York: Harper & Brothers, 1959), Vol. 2, p. 400. Also Franz Overbeck, quoted by Eduard Norden, *Die Antike Kunstprosa* (Leipzig: B. G. Teubner, 1909), p. 429: "Paul wrote to his churches only in order to tell them in writing what he would tell them orally if he were actually present in each case."

mostly Jewish in origins, but it was simply cast into Greek form.[14] The other viewpoint is best exemplified by Deissmann, who gave us a view of a harried Paul who dictated letters in spurts, ". . . without any careful arrangement, unconstrainedly passing from one thing to the other, often indeed jumping."[15]

We have begun to appreciate the fact that Paul did have a clear sense of the form of what he wanted to write. To speak of "Pauline letter form" is to speak of a normal progression of elements in the outline suggested. The formal outline is of course an external and internal form gained from letters which were in part rearranged and edited in the process of being collected;[16] a more inclusive outline might be given, but the one which we have sketched allows for all of the major recurrent elements. Reference to this probable outline does not mean that we assume that when Paul was writing or paused in his dictation, he thought, "Well, now, I've finished part 3.a—on to 3.b." Nor are we to assume that Paul decided which itemized sections taken together should comprise a letter to a particular situation, and then set about meeting such criteria. Rather, as Robert W. Funk noted earlier and reemphasized at the 1971 Society of Biblical Literature Seminar, "It is simply the way Paul writes letters."[17] It was the whole collocation of Paul's understanding of his task as apostle, along with the epistolary, sermonic, and religious-literary traditions of his Hellenistic and Jewish background which produced his letters. The elements in that collocation were Paul's driving insistence on his understanding of the Christian faith, his impatience with false interpretations of it, and his feeling for the way in which his churches would hear his letters. "Form," then, means not merely a sort of mechanical framework, but form is "the result of the entire, particular set of concrete circumstances and conditions which helped to shape the presentation of the literary work. . . ."[18]

14. Friedrich Köster, "Ob St. Paulus seine Sprache an der des Demosthenes gebildet habe?", *Theologische Studien und Kritiken* 27 (1854): 305–22.

15. Deissmann, *Paul*, p. 14.

16. See Walter Schmithals, "Die Thessalonicherbriefe als Briefkompositionen," in *Zeit und Geschichte*, ed. Erich Dinkler (Tübingen: J. C. B. Mohr [Paul Siebeck], 1964), pp. 314–15, esp. n. 40, where Schmithals rightly stresses that the redactor's arrangement was in the spirit of what Paul's own form was understood to be.

17. Robert W. Funk, *Language, Hermeneutic, and Word of God* (New York: Harper & Row, 1969), p. 270.

18. Herbert Mursurillo, S.J., "History and Symbol," *Theological Studies* 18 (1957): 363.

The advantages of having such a sense of Pauline form are manifold: it aids in our reconstruction of letters (such as the Corinthian or Philippian correspondence) which have been broken up and rearranged in transmission; it gives us a means of differentiating authentic from inauthentic letters; it gives us important insights into the structure of any particular letter, and hence enables interpretation of any part to be related to the whole; and it helps us to understand how Paul conceived of his writing letters in contrast to other literary modes. Attention to each major element of the Pauline letter form follows.

Opening. The initial formal segment of the letters has been studied in terms of its relationship to Jewish and Hellenistic epistolography. Some sort of consensus of views can be reported: Paul utilized both Graeco-Roman and Jewish elements; the literary form of the salutations is primarily Greek, but there are overtones resounding from Judaism. The standard "X to X, Greetings!" of Greek letters, followed by a formulaic expression of concern for the well-being of the addressee, is elaborated by Paul to include self-description ("an apostle of Christ Jesus by the will of God"), and often mention of his co-workers ("and from our brother Sosthenes"). Description of the addressees extends to mention of their special status as recipients of the gospel, as holy ones/saints, or as church groups in a particular region.

Scholars are divided about whether or not Paul was self-consciously playing with words when he replaced the normal "Greetings!" with his customary "Grace . . . and Peace. . . !" The Greek words *chairein* (greeting) and *charis* (grace) have linguistic similarity, and "Grace!" is not a common greeting-word in either Hellenistic or Jewish letters. On the other hand, "Peace!" (*shalom*) is a standard element of Jewish letter greetings, and there should be little doubt that Paul uses the term in conscious continuity with his Jewish heritage.[19]

The salutation, "Writer to Addressee, *chairein*," remained constant, with minor variations, from the third century B.C.E. to the third century C.E. in Graeco-Roman correspondence. Jewish letters, however, most often used a two-part salutation with the names of sender and addressee in the first part, and a prayer for peace and other blessings in the second: "Baruch the son of Neriah to the brethren carried into captivity: Mercy and Peace!" (Apoc. Bar.

19. See Werner Foerster, *Theological Dictionary of the New Testament* 2 (1964): 408, 411, 413.

78:2). The names in Jewish letters were more frequently embellished than in Greek letters.[20]

Normally Paul named himself as the sender of the letter, qualifying his name with some statement of his aposotolic authority to write letters. We ought to remember the interplay between Paul's sense of authority and his purposes in writing—more often than not, he intended to reprove or to improve the community to which he was writing, and hence it was important for him to establish his right to speak, his credentials, at the beginning of the letters. In several of the letters the bare statement of personal identification led him into theological reflection about being chosen as an apostle—cf. Romans, Galatians—and this sentiment breaks into the literary form of the opening.

Mention of Paul's co-workers (in Galatians it can extend to "all the brethren who are with me"!) is made, it seems to me, for a twofold reason: first, he wanted to establish that what he wrote derived not from his own fantasy, but from the developing Christian communities; second, the persons mentioned by name were often the trusted persons who were transmitting the letters and whose authority the addressees were to acknowledge. A very common feature in Hellenistic letters, mention of the carrier established the carrier's relationship to the writer, and guaranteed that what he had to say in interpreting the letter was authorized by the writer. The feature was especially important in Hellenistic letters where the actual information to be conveyed was trusted (only) to the messenger.

The opening part of Hellenistic letters included three parts, four on occasion: we have already mentioned the listing of addressees and writer with the greeting. This was very often followed by a health wish—a prayer for the addressee's well-being and often an indication of the writer's own good health. The health wish was usually followed by the supplication formula—an intercessory remark indicating that the writer was making supplication (*proskunema*) for the addressee before a god or before the gods; this

---

20. J. N. D. Kelly, *The Epistles of Peter and of Jude* (New York: Harper & Row, 1969), p. 39; on *chairein* greetings: Francis X. J. Exler, "The Form of the Ancient Greek Letter" (Diss., Catholic University of America, 1923), chart, p. 61. M. Luther Stirewalt, Jr. suggests in an unpublished paper, "The Letter from Paul to Philemon: The Letter-Setting," p. 4, that "the naming of multiple senders and recipients is a characteristic of official correspondence especially in Jewish communities. . . . The multiple senders stood ready to witness both to the fact that a letter had been written and to the content of the message. The multiple recipients bore witness to the fact that the letter had been officially received and read, and to its content."

formula became a fixed part of the Hellenistic letter during Roman times, although its origins reach back into Egyptian religious circles around Serapis. Finally, a fourth element (which could replace the third, supplication element) was the convention of stating that the writer held the addressee in his memory (the verb *mnemoneuein* in various combinations). This might be either a separate formula or an alternative to the supplication formula; in the Pauline letters it often appeared as the final clause of the thanksgiving period.[21]

Thanksgiving or Blessing. The second main section of the Pauline letter form has received more attention than any of the other parts. Paul Schubert, in *Form and Function of the Pauline Thanksgivings*, set major guidelines for the study of the thanksgiving unit; his lucid and important work has had much influence on epistolary research, even if scholars did not seem to recognize the methodological importance of the work until recently.

Hellenistic letters often have thanksgiving sections which state that the writer "gives thanks to the gods" or that the writer "makes continual mention of you before the gods," followed by the reasons that the gods are being thanked—usually because the gods have saved the writer or the addressee from some calamity. The form is found in 2 Macc. 1:11: ". . . having been saved by God out of grave dangers we thank him greatly for taking our side against the king." The thanksgiving or blessing form is used by Paul in all his letters except Galatians, where he was too concerned with the situation in the Galatian church to pause for the customary conventions. The opposite extreme is found in 1 Thessalonians, however, where it is possible to identify a full three-fifths of the letter as constituted by thanksgiving materials.[22]

John L. White argues in a recent paper (see above p. 22, n. 2) that Paul modified the Hellenistic thanksgiving statement in several ways: (a) the occasion for the thanksgiving is no longer being saved by the god(s) from great danger, but the occasion is often the faithfulness of the congregation to whom Paul is writing. (b) Paul tended to subsume the traditional prayer/intercession (making

---

21. Recent studies of these conventions are summarized by John L. White and Heikki Koskenniemi.

22. Paul Schubert, *Form and Function of the Pauline Thanksgivings*, Beihefte zur Zeitschrift für die Neutestamentliche Wissenschaft 20 (Berlin: Alfred Töpelmann, 1939), pp. 17, 24–26; and Eduard Lohse, *Colossians and Philemon*, trans. W. R. Poehlmann and R. J. Karris, ed. H. Koester (Philadelphia: Fortress Press, 1971), pp. 12–13, where there is a good listing of the major types of Pauline thanksgivings and examples from Hellenistic letters.

supplication for the addressee) into the thanksgiving period. So Paul expresses thanks for the current success of Christianity in the congregation addressed, and his supplication is that the good state of affairs will be continued.[23] The thanksgiving period also functions as a sort of shorthand indicator of the contents of particular Pauline letters, as Schubert originally suggested.[24]

Beda Rigaux thinks that Paul began his preaching with a thanksgiving, a practice he then carried over into his correspondence. If this was the case, it explains why the thanksgivings are not cast entirely into the sentiment of giving thanks *for* something, but also include admonitions and begin to argue that a particular course of action is required by the situation; or as Paul Schubert put it, "All Pauline thanksgivings have either explicitly or implicity paraenetic function."[25]

Contrary to Schubert, however, the main line of research on the thanksgivings has stressed the liturgical aspects of the thanksgivings rather than the specifically paraenetic aspects. There is close correspondence between opening thanksgiving phrases that have to do with giving thanks or blessing and Hellenistic-Jewish formulae of thanks and praise, and what has been previously identified as the "thanksgiving" on the basis of comparison with this feature of Greek letters must now be fully identified as the "thanksgiving and/or blessing" segment.

The major presentation of the data is by James M. Robinson, whose conclusions and observations have been supported by most

23. White, "The Structural Analysis of Philemon," pp. 30–33; he illustrates from Philemon: "The cause of thanksgiving in Philemon . . . is the report of Philemon's love and faith for the Lord Jesus and for all the saints. The corresponding prayer . . . is that the fellowship of his faith will extend to a knowledge of every good thing for Christ." See also Schubert, *Form and Function of the Pauline Thanksgivings*, pp. 167–68, and Lohse, *Colossians and Philemon*, pp. 24 ff., 31.

24. See Schubert, *Form and Function of the Pauline Thanksgivings*, p. 24 and compare White, "The Structural Analysis of Philemon," p. 32: "The thanksgiving, like the salutation, signals—prior to the actual disclosure of the subject matter of the letter in the body—the reason for writing." The importance of recognizing this form is stressed by Robert Jewett, "The Epistolary Thanksgivings and the Integrity of Philippians," *Novum Testamentum* 12 (1970): 53: "Despite the abrupt transitions, the entire letter as it now stands is the product of the author's intention set forth in the epistolary thanksgiving." See also Lohse, *Colossians and Philemon*, p. 92, n. 5.

25. Schubert, *Form and Function of the Pauline Thanksgivings*, p. 89, cf. pp. 105 f., 115 f.; Beda Rigaux, *Letters of St. Paul: Modern Studies*, trans. S. Yonick (Chicago: Franciscan Herald Press, 1968), p. 122; and Lohse, *Colossians and Philemon*, p. 94, n. 13 and pp. 14 ff.

subsequent writers.[26] Robinson suggested that one can trace, within the tradition history of primitive Christianity, a definite preference for formulae of thanksgiving rather than blessing; the thanksgiving formulae acquire an epistolary meaning of such importance that their lack betokens significant information about any particular letter situation. The thanksgiving is frequently tied to the success of primitive Christianity—especially in contrast to Judaism—and indicates the growing sense of identity of the Christian movement; the latter replaced Jewish formulae of blessing with Christian formulae of thanksgiving. Paul generally gives thanks that things are going well, and sees this as evidence of the power of God working through the churches as it had worked through the synagogue. The thanksgiving can also modulate into the form of a blessing[27] and it frequently has an eschatological climax—the present time of thanksgiving is linked with the final days of the supreme rule of God.

Scholars have noted that the thanksgivings summarize and announce the contents of the letters, as we indicated. Fred O. Francis has recently pursued this phenomenon by drawing in Hellenistic and especially Hellenistic-Jewish epistolary literature. He suggests that we may trace a progression of development of the thanksgiving/blessing formula: (a) there are successive stages of the statement marked off by "blessing" or "rejoicing" (Josephus, Eupolemus, Philemon 4–7); then (b) an alternate form found in 1 Macc. 10:25–45; (c) thanksgiving section (1, 2 Thess.) or thanksgiving with rejoicing section (Phil.) which structure the entire body of the letter; (d) blessing and thanksgiving paired to frame the opening statement at the beginning and end (2 Cor.); (e) the opening statement initiated and carried forward by combinations of blessings and thanksgivings (Eph.), by a pair of thanksgivings (Col.) or a pair of rejoicing formulae (3 John); and finally (f) structure of the letter determined by double thanksgiving formulae, though not introduced with traditional technical terms (Josephus, 1 John).[28]

26. James M. Robinson, "Die Hodajot-Formel in Gebet und Hymnus des Frühchristentums," in *Apophoreta: Festschrift für Ernst Haenchen*, ed. W. Eltester and F. H. Kettler (Berlin: Alfred Töpelmann, 1964), pp. 194–235; cf. "The Historicality of Biblical Language," in *The Old Testament and Christian Faith*, ed. B. W. Anderson (New York: Harper & Row, 1963), pp. 124–58. See also Nils Dahl, "Adresse und Proömium des Epheserbriefes," *Theologische Zeitschrift* 7 (1951): 250 ff.

27. Rigaux, *Letters of St. Paul*, pp. 120–21, suggests the sequence of faith, hope, and charity.

28. Fred O. Francis, "The Form and Function of the Opening and Closing Paragraphs of James and I John," *Zeitschrift für die Neutestamentliche Wissen-*

Body. Oddly enough, the actual part of the Pauline letter in which Paul dealt with issues most directly and at length, the body, has received least attention with respect to its formal elements. Of course most Pauline exegesis and theological analysis has had to deal with material in the bodies of the letters, but there is little specific formal analysis of the body section as a whole. The reasons for this lack of attention may be explained in several ways: the body as a formal entity has not been recognized as sufficiently unitary or consistent from letter to letter to reward formal analysis; there is the difficulty of identifying how the "normative" forms of the body took shape; there is the difficulty seen in several attempts to define where the body sections begin and end; and finally there is confusion because of several letters (1 Cor., Phil., 2 Thess.) in which the body seems almost entirely assimilated to the thanksgiving. Parts of the body, however, have been intensively analyzed.

Several possible openings of the body have been identified.

(a) Jack T. Sanders, extending Schubert's work on thanksgiving sections by identifying their closing formulae, notes the regularity with which a formula of *request* or *appeal* or *injunction* opens the main segment of the letter. Following a conjunction, a verb of request or appeal (especially *parakalo,* "I appeal . . .") appears, followed by the vocative case, often an appeal to the authority of the Lord, and then the content of the request. The formula is not restricted to the closings of the thanksgivings, but functions "to introduce new material, to change the subject of discussion, or when the argument takes a new tack." According to John L. White, the request formula is best understood in relation to the polite entreaties of official petitions.[29]

(b) A second possible opening is the formula of *disclosure:* "I want you to know that . . ." or "I do not want you to be ignorant . . ." (Rom. 1:13, 2 Cor. 1:8, 1 Thess. 2:1, Phil. 1:12, Gal. 1:11; compare 1 Cor. 11:3, 1 Thess. 4:13, 1 Cor. 10:1, 12:1, Rom. 11:25). This formula counsels the addressees or informs them about a certain subject; both of these formulae provide headings for the following

schaft 61 (1970): 110–26. The major theme of the article is the identification of a "double introduction" formula which was "an epistolary form available to the Hellenistic letter writer."

29. Sanders, "The Transition from Opening Epistolary Thanksgiving," p. 349; White, "The Structural Analysis of Philemon," pp. 23 f., and "Introductory Formulae in the Body of the Pauline Letter," *JBL* 90 (1971): 93; compare Philem. 8 ff., 1 Cor. 1:10.

paragraph(s) and state briefly its content, analogous to a news-paper headline and subtitle.[30]

(c) *Joy* formulae ("I rejoice greatly that . . .") were usually occasioned by receipt of good news about the addressee.[31] The joy formula occasionally introduced the body of the Greek letter; the writer's joy was occasioned by having received correspondence from the addressee, or by having heard of the recovery or the good health of the addressee. Such joy expressions in Greek letters were often veiled requests to the addressee to write more!—more letters will provide more occasions to be joyous. The formula is reflected in Philemon: Paul was joyous that Philemon's development in Christianity had gone smoothly. Here the joy formula elides with a request formula; Paul proceeded to make an elaborate, long request of Philemon that is strikingly extended, by Greek standards.[32]

(d) Expressions of *astonishment* ("I am amazed that . . .") could also introduce the body of letters—astonishment at the addressee's failure to write, usually as a means of evoking an epistolary reply, but in the Pauline use, Gal. 1:6, it refers not to the failure to write, but to the Galatians' apparent rejection of the gospel.

(e, f) Finally, formulae of *compliance* and of *hearing* or *learning* were used. The former reminded the addressees of their obligations or reported compliance with instructions (compare Gal. 1:9); the latter were used when the writer sought elucidation of secondhand news or gossip (compare Gal. 1:13 f.).[33]

Within the bodies of the Pauline letters, consistent use of formulae seems less likely—or at any rate no such consistent use has been identified. My own feeling is that in the body sections of the longer letters, at least, Paul had more inclination to strike out on his own and to be least bound by epistolary structures. Comparative materials might include the letter-essays, whose internal bodies cannot be said to have a particular formal structure, or preaching

---

30. Sanders, "The Transition from Opening Epistolary Thanksgiving," p. 344; see also Terence Y. Mullins, "Disclosure: A Literary Form in the New Testament," *Novum Testamentum* 4 (1964): 44–50.

31. White, "Introductory Formulae in the Body of the Pauline Letter," p. 94; see Phil. 4:10, Philemon 7. White lists the formulae on pp. 95–96.

32. White, "The Structural Analysis of Philemon," p. 37, notes how the request is anticipated in the salutation and thanksgiving.

33. White, "Introductory Formulae in the Body of the Pauline Letter," pp. 94–95, with examples from papyri.

traditions in the Hellenistic world. For formal analysis we must turn to structural or sequence analysis as well as to stylistic elements. Here we must look for subforms (see the next chapter) and characteristic means of expression rather than influences from pre-Pauline letter forms.

Materials coming at the close of the body segment have been analyzed. Paul's tendency to attach eschatological conclusions to his discussions (Rom. 8:31–39, 11:25–36, 1 Cor. 4:6–13, 2 Cor. 6:1 ff. (?), Gal. 6:7–10, Phil. 2:14–18, 1 Thess. 2:13–16) has been discussed by Robert W. Funk,[34] as has the travelogue form which Paul developed into his own special formula, called by Funk the "apostolic parousia." This element consists of the sections of the letters in which "Paul often indicates his reason for or disposition in writing, his intention or hope to dispatch an emissary, and his intention or hope to pay the congregation a personal visit.[35] The underlying theme of such sections (Rom. 15:14–33, Philem. 21 f., 1 Cor. 4:14–21, 1 Thess. 2:17–3:13, 2 Cor. 12:14–13:13, Gal. 4:12–20, Phil. 2:19–24) is "the presence of apostolic authority and power —of which the travelogue in the narrow sense is only one element."[36] The emphasis upon "presence" is likely a carry-over from the Greek letter tradition; we mentioned above that *parousia* (presence) was taken by Koskenniemi to represent one of the three central aspects of Greek correspondence. Paul thought of his presence with the groups he addressed as conveying not just personal authority, but *apostolic* authority and hence power; in these segments of his letters, we sense Paul's understanding of the epistolary situation as generally understood in the Graeco-Roman world as well as his understanding of his personal status in the churches. He wrote letters to function as substitute communications necessitated by his spatial distance from his churches. Paul's natural way of being with the congregations is in person—hence the element Funk identifies as the apostolic parousia suggests the compromise Paul finally reached. Unable to be present in person, his letters were a direct substitute, and were to be accorded weight equal to Paul's physical presence.

34. Funk, *Language, Hermeneutic, and Word of God*, pp. 217, 264–65, 269.

35. Robert W. Funk, "The Apostolic *Parousia*: Form and Significance," in *Christian History and Interpretation: Studies Presented to John Knox*, ed. W. R. Farmer, C. F. D. Moule, and R. R. Niebuhr (Cambridge: The University Press, 1967), p. 249.

36. Ibid.

We also gain a sense of the importance of his emissaries or letter carriers: they receive authority to convey the letters, to expand upon them, and to continue Paul's work.

John L. White draws Funk's travelogue/apostolic parousia into connection with the body closings of papyri letters, which he dissects into two or three formal features: statement of the motivation of writing the letter, or a reaction-oriented "responsibility" phrase urging response to the information presented in the body of the letter, and mention of an anticipated visit or proposed further exchange of letters.[37] In Philemon, Galatians, and Romans, corresponding units are found: first Paul states the motivation for writing, combined in each case with a responsibility phrase; this is followed by a formula expressing confidence in the addressees; and finally there is mention of the anticipated visit, which may be called[38] the apostolic parousia on the basis of its internal content.

Especially in the post-Pauline letters this section—which is less clearly a distinct letter section—becomes the locus for exchange of plans, appeals for cooperation in missionary work (cf. 2 Tim. 4:9 ff.), or recommendation of carriers (cf. Eph. 6:21–22 and Col. 4:7–9).

Paraenesis. One of the most important reclamation projects in the history of biblical research was the reclaiming of Paul as a situational or contextualist theologian and ethicist rather than as a dogmatic moralist. Instead of visualizing Paul as an abstract thinker spinning webs of ethical and moral duties, modern interpretors see him as involved with his addressees in the process of dialogic piecing-together of concrete ethical responses in each situation. Often it is almost impossible to interpret Paul correctly until we have gained some sense of the background of the community to which he is writing; and interpretation has come to focus not so much upon a supposed internal consistency in Pauline thought as upon his resilience and his ability to explore the possible contours of the Christian religious life in different historical contexts.

Paraenetic materials, however, are by and large traditional materials: they arise out of community life and thought, and tend to be consistently conservative. When certain sections of the letters are formally of a paraenetic nature, then, we should expect those parts to be the locations where Paul most relies upon his background and

37. White, "The Structural Analysis of Philemon," pp. 38–39.
38. White (ibid., p. 44), agreeing with Funk.

training to supplement and to support his contextualism.[39] And when attention is focused upon the post-Pauline letters, an even greater use of pre- and non-Christian paraenetic forms is found.[40]

To study Paul's ethical teaching materials is to study his preaching, since one may conclude with Thyen[41] that the Jewish sermon was always aimed at practical-paraenetic goals. The influence of the Jewish sermonic tradition upon Paul is beginning to be seen as a generic influence working in his head along with the popular philosophical street preaching of the Hellenistic world.[42] Neither tradition dominated the man; but we can say that Paul's preaching was influenced by both traditions, and further that the two traditions have contributed indirectly to the ways Paul went about *writing* paraenetic matter.

Paul utilized traditional materials of several types—materials from the Old Testament and other Jewish literature, as well as the substance of Hellenistic moral traditions—but he did not conceive of himself as building a new moral code or as collecting a new set of ethical maxims.[43] His paraenetic materials are not always tightly interwoven with other reflections and advice to Christian communities, but nonetheless they are interwoven, and the important thing is to understand the care with which Paul has utilized and modified his source materials.[44]

39. The paraenetic sections also indicate something of the genre of the primitive Christian letters; paraenetic material is "literary" in a way that other materials are not, and inclusion of such materials therefore discloses lines of contact with "literary" rather than "common" or popular letter trajectories. In making this point, Funk (*Language, Hermeneutic, and Word of God*, p. 256) does not mean to imply that paraenetic materials are not related to oral modes of presentation—teaching, catechesis, sermon, etc.—for they clearly are. See especially Hartwig Thyen, *Der Stil der Jüdisch-Hellenistischen Homilie* (Göttingen: Vandenhoeck & Ruprecht, 1955), p. 85.
40. Compare stylistic elements such as the athletic contest in 1 Cor. 9:24–27, the teaching of the Two Ways in Didache and Barnabas, and the discussion of the lists of vices and virtues and the catalogues of household duties in chap. 3.
41. Thyen, *Der Stil der Jüdisch-Hellenistischen Homilie*, p. 87.
42. See Wilhelm Wuellner, "Haggadic Homily Genre in I Corinthians 1–3," *JBL* 9 (1970): 199–204; Rudolf Bultmann, *Der Stil der paulinischen Predigt und die kynisch-stoische Diatribe* (Göttingen: Vandenhoeck & Ruprecht, 1910); Thyen, *Der Stil der Jüdisch-Hellenistischen Homilie*; and Maurice Jones, "The Style of Paul's Preaching," *Expositor* 14 (1917): 241–58, 330–47.
43. See Victor P. Furnish, *Theology and Ethics in Paul* (Nashville: Abingdon Press, 1968), esp. chap. 2.
44. With Furnish (*Theology and Ethics in Paul*, p. 260), against the view of Martin Dibelius that paraenetic materials were not carefully chosen or ordered, and entirely different from the "theological" or "kerygmatic" sections of the letters; see Martin Dibelius, *From Tradition to Gospel*, trans. B. L. Woolf (New York: Charles Scribner's Sons, n.d.), chap. 9.

(b) Dictation and methods of composition. I am not as convinced as some writers that we may identify the manner in which Paul composed his letters. Certainly there is less inclination today to accept Deissmann's judgment that they were dashed off "amid the storm and stress of his wandering life."[53] Remarks in the Pauline letters about the process of writing can be interpreted several ways (Rom. 16:22, 1 Cor. 16:21, Gal. 6:11, 2 Thess. 3:17, Philemon 19).

Rather than attempting to prove that Paul did or did not use secretaries—I think he did—it seems more helpful to explore the alternatives available to him. In addition to writing letters in one's own handwriting (which might be copied into a copybook by oneself or by a secretary), three alternatives seem most likely: (i) dictation to a secretary, word by word, or even syllable by syllable; (ii) dictation of the sense of the message, leaving the formulation of the material to the secretary; or (iii) instruction of a secretary or friend to write in one's name, without indication of specific contents.[54] Whichever method Paul used, assuming that he mostly used an agent other than himself, it was not unusual for him to add a statement in his own handwriting. In Hellenistic official letter records the writer of a letter might add a resume of the document in his own handwriting, indicating that he was aware of its contents and details. Such a situation is suggested by Philemon 19, where Paul's usual "I, Paul, write this (i.e., this part) with my own hand" is immediately followed by his restating his willingness to assume Onesimus's debts to Philemon ("I will repay it . . .").

Paul makes a point of indicating those who are especially close to him when writing his letters (1 Cor. 1:1, 2 Cor. 1:1, Phil. 1:1, 1 Thess. 1:1, Philemon 1, and compare Col. 1:1 and 2 Thess. 1:1), and it may be that these co-workers contributed substantial parts of the letters' contents.

(c) Holy Kiss. In several of the letters (Rom. 16:16, 1 Cor. 16:20, 2 Cor. 13:12, 1 Thess. 5:26) Paul gives instruction to greet one another with a holy kiss. I do not know of formal studies of this con-

53. Deissmann, *Paul*, pp. 13–14; Deissmann used this as an explanation of the abrupt changes of mood in the letters.

54. See also Gordon J. Bahr, "Paul and Letter Writing in the Fifth Century," *Catholic Biblical Quarterly* 28 (1966): 465–77. The article explores the possible uses of secretaries and means of transcription in antiquity, and supplies many references to these features. See also Joseph Fitzmyer, "New Testament Epistles," *The Jerome Biblical Commentary*, ed. R. E. Brown et al. (Englewood Cliffs: Prentice-Hall, Inc., 1968), p. 226, and earlier literature discussed by Rigaux, *Letters of St. Paul*, p. 234, n. 7.

vention, but we may note that it usually appears in or just preceding the closing statement, and that it reflects once again the liturgical setting of the letters.

(d) Closing Greetings to a List of People. The convention found in Rom. 16:3 f. (compare Col. 4:10 ff.) is well documented from the papyri, although the list in Romans 16 is strikingly extended.[55]

SUMMARY AND OBSERVATIONS: THE PAULINE LETTERS

Certain features of the Pauline correspondence have now come into view, and may be summarized vis-à-vis Hellenistic letter traditions:

1. *Form.* The Pauline letters are briefer and less stereotyped in phraseology than Hellenistic letters; Paul surely had his own favorite epistolary phrases, but there is more differentiation between any of several of his letters than between hundreds of Hellenistic letters. We have indicated that the structural form of the Pauline letters can be charted, although the divisions suggested are open to correction as we gain greater precision in evaluating primitive Christian correspondence in the light of its Hellenistic contemporaries. A listing of the main Pauline letters with formal parts identified in chart form will be found on the facing page; identification of formal parts is often tentative, since delineation of the ending of one formal part, such as the thanksgiving, and the beginning of another, such as the body-opening, is still in dispute.

2. *Content.* The letter form which developed in the Pauline letters was richer than either the brief private letters or the more developed letter-essays of Hellenism. Paul's letters deal with complex relationships between Christian church members in terms of their new understandings of life (religion) rather than primarily in terms of cultivating friendly relationships or providing instruction. While there are many times when the Pauline letters do function to maintain friendly relationships, their purpose goes beyond that; Paul sought to bring his addressees into richer experiences of the new religion, to move them to new heights of action and response, not merely to improve or maintain relationships to himself. The letters incorporate elements of the ongoing life of the churches such as liturgical materials, sacred traditions, legal and moral guidelines, and sayings.

55. See Henry G. Meecham, *Light from Ancient Letters* (London: George Allen & Unwin, Ltd., 1923), p. 115; John G. Winter, *Life and Letters in the Papyri* (Ann Arbor: University of Michigan Press, 1933), p. 87; and Mullins, "Greeting as a New Testament Form," p. 425.

FORMAL PARTS OF THE PAULINE LETTERS

	Rom.	1 Cor.	2 Cor.	Gal.	Phil.	1 Thess.	Philem.
OPENING							
a. sender	1:1	1:1	1:1	1:1–2	1:1	1:1	v. 1–3
b. addressee	1:7	1:2	1:1	1:2	1:1	1:1	1–2
c. greeting	1:7b	1:3	1:2	1:3	1:2	1:1	3
THANKSGIVING/ BLESSING	1:8–17	1:4–9	1:3+	missing	1:3–11	1:2–16	3–11
intercession	1:9–10		(Cf. 13:7, 9)		1:9–11	(Cf. 3:10)	6
eschatological climax		1:8–9, 4:5			1:10–11	1:10, 3:11–13	6
BODY	1:13–8:39	1:10–4:21	1:8–2:13, 7:5–6, 2:14–7:4, 10:1–13:14	1:6–5:16 (–6:17?)	1:12–2:30	2:1–3:13	8–22
a. formal opening	1:13–15	1:10–16	1:8–12	1:6–14	1:12–18	2:1–4 (–12?)	7–14
b. eschatological conclusion	8:31–39, 11:25–36	4:6–13	missing or 6:1 ff.	6:7–10	2:14–18	2:13–16	21–22
c. travelogue	15:14–33	4:14–21	12:14–13:13	4:12–20	2:19–24	2:17–3:13	21–22
PARAENESIS	12:13, 12:1–15:13	missing		5:13–6:10	missing	4:1–12, 5:1–22	cf. 21
CLOSING							
a. greetings	16:3–16, 23	16:19–21	13:12–13		4:21–22	5:26	23–25
b. doxology	16:25–27			1:5	4:20	5:23	
c. benediction	15:33, 16:20	16:23	12:14	6:18	4:22	5:28	25

3. *Epistolary Situations.* Paul was concerned with the life situations of the addressees, but never in the impersonal way characteristic of Hellenistic letters. Paul sent information about his own health and circumstances from time to time, but might depend upon the carrier to convey such information. Instead of impersonal phrases, rich in etiquette and convention, Paul threw himself into his letters with emotions bared.[56] The letters arose in response to reports from specific contexts, and Paul treated each situation as unique and important; he was not so much forging religious dogma as conveying his understanding of how Christianity might be structured in the concrete situational contexts of the particular addressees.

4. *Authority.* Paul wrote as a specifically empowered leader of the church—in his understanding, he wrote as an apostle. He was touchy about his right to administer apostolic authority, and made a point of his apostolicity in every letter. His wishes were meant to be obeyed since they had the authority of eschatological revelation. To some extent the Pauline letters bore the teaching authority of Hellenistic letters of Epicurus or Apollonius; but Paul did not see his authority as arbitrary or capricious—rather he made careful attempts to listen to his own preaching in order to be sure that it was in line with authentic Christian tradition.[57]

5. *Oral Character.* The Pauline letters were at best a makeshift substitute for Paul's presence with the addressees. The inclusion of the travelogue may be an influence from Hellenistic letters; but in Paul's letters it stands as an element reminding us that Paul would rather have conveyed his information in person than in letters. His letters implied an open future: until Paul could be with the addressees, he presumed to give them encouragement and advice. Since the letters were composed of what Paul wanted to say orally, there was no restricting formula for writing letters any more than

56. Stirewalt, "A Survey of the Uses of Letter-Writing," p. 10, suggests that Paul's impersonal use of stereotyped phrases was due to his need to write letters rather than being able to enjoy personal contact. I am more inclined to explain it on the basis of limited education and what might be called the awe of writing in antiquity. Nonetheless there is in Paul an impatience with writing; Günther Bornkamm, *Paul,* trans. D. M. G. Stalker (New York: Harper & Row, 1971), p. xxii, is correct in pointing to 1 Thess. 2:17 f. and Rom. 15:22 ff., and speaking of Paul's letters "as makeshifts, an unsatisfactory substitute for a personal meeting which was no longer, or not yet, possible."

57. See Funk, *Language, Hermeneutic, and Word of God,* chap. 11, "Word and Word in I Corinthians 2:6–16."

there was any one standard preaching formula, and the Pauline letters display a natural and unstudied diversity. Paul was not writing literature in the book sense; he was writing what he wished he could say in person, and traits of his oral presentation come through from time to time.[58]

6. *Lost Letters.* The letters are artifacts of interchanges, some of them quite involved, between Paul and the addressees (even in Romans, where instead of arguing with the addressees, whom he has not met, he argues with standard positions of those who rejected his theology). Although various attempts have been made to identify the letters "behind" the letters in the present Pauline corpus, we cannot definitely reconstruct anything more than probable quotes in Paul's letters when he takes up a phrase from a letter addressed to him and expands or refutes it (especially in the Corinthian correspondence).

7. *Style.* The language and style of Paul's letters reflect neither the flat, graceless papyrus letters nor rhetorically polished elements of the treatise or public letter. Rhetorical influences are present, but Paul frequently breaks into the rhetorical structure with exclamations, quotations, and additional observations. His use of visual imagery and situational analogies depends more often upon his own adaptations of such materials than upon conventional associations.[59]

8. *Messengers.* We have noted the late-Hellenistic tendency to send the real message along with the trusted carrier rather than including it in the letter—mainly because of political intrigue and the insecurity of the postal system. The early Christian carriers were trustworthy, usually private individuals able to carry and expand upon the letters, and I often have the sense that Paul, who made such a point of indicating his trust in the carriers (co-workers), did

---

58. Elements of the Cynic-Stoic diatribe are found in the letters, as detailed in Bultmann, *Der Stil der paulinischen Predigt;* he concludes that there are few direct influences, many general allusions. Hartwig Thyen, *Der Stil der Jüdisch-Hellenistischen Homilie,* has shown how the diatribic type of exhortation was present in diaspora Judaism. G. Stählin, "Zum Gebrauch von Beteuerungs-formeln," *Novum Testamentum* 5 (1962): 115–43, elucidates the frequent use of swearing that one's message was God-given.

59. Hence the importance of identifying the possible historical meanings of any particular image, as well as determining which specific application Paul may be making in the particular context. See Herbert W. Gale, *The Use of Analogy in the Letters of Paul* (Philadelphia: Westminster Press, 1964), who notes that Paul may use a cluster of images to make a single point, or he may drop one image to pick up another before exhausting the possibilities of the first; the points Paul makes are not always consistent with the actual situations from which the analogies are derived.

not think of his written letters as exhausting what he wished to communicate. He thought of his associates, especially those commissioned to carry his letters, as able to extend his own teachings.[60] I wonder if the Pauline letters may not be seen as the essential part of the messages Paul had to convey, pressed into brief compass as a basis for elaboration by the carriers. The subsequent reading of the letters in the primitive Christian communities would then have been the occasions for full exposition and expansion of the sketch of material in the letters.

9. *Collections.* The collection of the Pauline letters we now possess came about as a fortuitous accident of fate. Or at least we hope it was fortuitous, since we do not know what else Paul may have written, and must base our opinions on the extant letters. The collection of Pauline letters probably occurred within a decade or so of their composition. Since the letters were written to early Christian communities, and were read aloud during the meetings of these communities, eventually becoming a part of the formal liturgy of the Christian worship, it may be that the first collections were made to satisfy needs for worship. An additional stimulus may well have been the need for practical advice and instruction; especially in the later generations of the church, when dissension and problems of right belief were prominent, collections of the letters may have been made as a means of regaining the supposed wholeness and peace of the earliest church. Paul came to be seen as the great model from the first generations of the church, and his letters were assumed to speak to all generations of the church (see chap. 4, pp. 67–69).[61]

10. *Redaction.* The problem of rearrangement and dislocation of the Pauline letters as well as the extent to which they have been

---

60. This feature is pronounced in the post-Pauline letters closest to the genuine Pauline epistles, namely, in Ephesians and Colossians; could it be that the post-Pauline writers were so conscious of this habit that they sought to emphasize it in the letters they wrote? Compare Eph. 6:21-22, "Tychicus the beloved brother and faithful minister in the Lord will tell you everything. I have sent him to you for this very purpose, that you may know how we are, and that he may encourage your hearts," and Col. 4:7-8, "Tychicus will tell you about my affairs . . . I have sent him . . . that you may know how we are and that he may encourage your hearts, and with him Onesimus. . . ."

61. Edgar J. Goodspeed, *New Solutions of New Testament Problems* (Chicago: University of Chicago Press, 1927), *The Formation of the New Testament* (Chicago: University of Chicago Press, 1926), and Lucretta Mowry, "The Early Circulation of Paul's Letters," *JBL* 64 (1945), argue that the publication of the Pauline corpus accounts for the first extensive influence of Paul in the churches, as well as acting as a spur for post-Pauline literary production.

edited or redacted is beyond the scope of this volume; details are available in technical New Testament introductions and commentaries. It is probably impossible to determine the extent to which possession of additional genuine letters might influence our understanding of Paul's thought. If the letters were collected for liturgical and teaching purposes (as suggested in #9), redactors were no doubt especially concerned to highlight (and possibly to create) materials to satisfy those uses.

III

Forms within the
New Testament Epistles

So far we have given a brief summary of the types of epistolary intercourse in the Hellenistic world (chapter one) and an indication of the overall form which Paul utilized in his letters (chapter two). In this chapter the focus of our attention is somewhat more restricted. Here we are especially interested in the small subunits found within the primitive Christian letters.

Research materials on the subforms can be fairly readily organized into categories: it is mostly a mechanical matter to identify the work that has been done on the various subunits of formal materials such as confessional formulae, petitions, catechetical statements, and the like. But before reviewing this research, we must seek greater clarification about the general objectives of such literary inquiry, especially since the history of epistolary research betrays confusion. Scholars have especially confused levels and types of materials, seeking stylistic traits (such as kerygmatic preaching) as well as formal ones, and sometimes confusing traditional rhetoric with personal style.

Anyone who attempts to formulate a comprehensive mode of approach to such a large body of materials might appear to possess rather foolhardy confidence. Nevertheless, understanding of the primitive Christian literature will be clarified if future studies pay more careful attention to the literary features of the materials they analyze. Methodologically, at least, differentiations ought to be made between: (a) stylistic and rhetorical features, (b) structural features, (c) formal and generic traits, and (d) use of traditional materials, including traditional forms and styles.

Stylistic and Rhetorical Features. Attention to style and rhetoric has not been a regular feature of New Testament criticism since the time of the late nineteenth-century scholars such as Eduard Norden and Paul Wendland, whose academic training included strong emphasis on classical literature. I know of few New Testament scholars at the present time who can bring to bear upon the development of the Christian literature a fully comprehensive knowledge of classical literature. There are, to be sure, excellent analyses of the relationships between figures of classical antiquity and New Testament writings,[1] but by and large New Testament studies have become so all-encompassing that no individual can adequately treat both classical and early Christian developments.

One consequence of this situation is that few contemporary studies display the sensitivity toward the stylistic and rhetorical features of biblical literature which was found in earlier scholarship. A few studies of specific rhetorical traits (such as chiasm) are available, but there are no adequate studies comparing primitive Christian literary production with that of antiquity. One important task for the study of primitive Christian literature should be to renew acquaintance with classical studies and literary criticism.[2]

Rhetorical features in Paul can be roughly divided into literary devices and oratorical devices: to the former belong the use of parallelism and/or antithesis familiar from the Israelite literature (flesh and spirit, letter and spirit), chiastic development (in which themes are treated in the pattern *abc–cba*), paradoxical and metaphoric imagery and development, and the use of grouping of items for dramatic effect (pleonasm, as Gal. 4:10, "You observe days, and months, and seasons, and years!"). Oratorical influences in Paul and the other letter writers include "preaching style" (address or direct questions to persons in the audience, solemn and elaborate references to God), homiletic directness (Rom. 14:12, "So let each of us give account of himself to God"), anacolutha (changes of grammatical construction within one sentence unit—2 Cor. 1:23, "But

---

1. Such as Hans Dieter Betz, *Lukian von Samosata und das Neue Testament* (Berlin: Academie-Verlag, 1961).

2. Three recent books demonstrate how the resources of literary criticism and rhetoric can enrich our understandings of biblical material: Amos N. Wilder, *Early Christian Rhetoric: The Language of the Gospel*, new ed. (Cambridge: Harvard University Press, 1971); William A. Beardslee, *Literary Criticism of the New Testament*, in the same series as this volume (Philadelphia: Fortress Press, 1970); and Dan O. Via, Jr., *The Parables: Their Literary and Existential Dimension* (Philadelphia: Fortress Press, 1967).

I call God to witness against me—it was to spare you . . ."), meiosis (litotes: use of a negative expression to convey a positive meaning, 1 Cor. 1:25, "For the foolishness of God is wiser than men, and the weakness of God is stronger than men"), formulaic summaries, and rhythmic expression. Studies of Pauline and post-Pauline diction and imagery are also relevant.[3]

These features appear primarily as means of enriching expression, and involve use of traditional patterns of expression, as well as the stylistic characteristics of a particular writer. "Style" is one of the most debatable terms in literary criticism, and clarity in its use in biblical studies appears to be an almost unattainable desideratum; but the emphasis upon biblical theology in this century must now be supplemented by stylistic analysis to a much greater extent if we are to comprehend fully the epistolary literature of primitive Christianity.

Rhetorical criticism of our day is no longer restricted to the usual studies of tropes and figures of speech, but may be understood as treating structure as well. How a particular writer organizes his thoughts and expresses them, in what characteristic sequences he writes, and how he conceives of the impact of his writing are all valid concerns of the rhetorical critic.[4]

Structural Features. The second group of literary features, which I have called structural features, overlaps with the first group; the difference in groupings is meant to stress only that the first group includes primarily features of individual traits and characteristic ways of using language; this second set of features is thought of more in terms of the ways large units of material are organized by an author, and of course it overlaps in turn with the third group, formal features. Structural features may be identified apart from formal features, however, if we think of form as something more long-range and continuous than structure; e.g., the normal pattern

3. See Beda Rigaux, *Letters of St. Paul: Modern Studies,* trans. S. Yonick (Chicago: Franciscan Herald Press, 1968), pp. 126–29 and 133 (with bibliography in the notes), and H. W. Gale, *The Use of Analogy in the Letters of Paul* (Philadelphia: Westminster Press, 1964).

4. David Greenwood, "Rhetorical Criticism and Formgeschichte. Some Methodological Considerations," *JBL* 89 (1970): 418–26, stresses structural analysis as constitutive of rhetorical criticism to a greater extent than I think necessary, although he and John L. White, "The Structural Analysis of Philemon: A Point of Departure in the Formal Analysis of the Pauline Letter" (photocopy for the Society of Biblical Literature Seminar on the Form and Function of the Pauline Letters, 1971), both urge the benefits of structural analysis for biblical research.

of Pauline letters is formal—traditional or habitual to Paul—whereas the particular arrangement of units of material within a formal section or for a particular unit of material may be referred to as the structure of the passage or passages.

Structure also includes the important rearrangements of materials performed by editors, collectors, and redactors. In attempting to discern how a letter which now appears as an extremely complex intermixture of letter fragments may have appeared originally, a literary sequence analysis can be suggested—we attempt to identify how the original structure of the letter was conceived. Given such identification according to stylistic and formal features, and according to the flow of thought in the (supposed) original letter, we are often able, as in the Corinthian correspondence, to suggest how the materials have come into their present order, and to identify the original strands of the materials.

Structural analysis is also important when it comes to identifying the ways an author has organized his subject before coming to write; he may, for instance, make concessions to his readers as a basis for pressing his own demands upon them. If an author's sense of structural arrangement is kept in mind, it will be possible to suggest which portions of the writing are more and which less important; aware of an author's usual structural arrangement, the contemporary reader stands much closer to the original writer at the point of first composition.

Attention to structure also discloses the ways in which a letter writer weights particular epistolary elements which may be shared with the tradition. Our attention to formal elements must be supplemented in each case with attention to the specific manner in which a writer has utilized them. "Formulae," notes John L. White, "are a helpful device for uncovering the internal logic of the letter, generally, but the meaning of a formula in any specific instance must be determined on the internal contours of the letter itself."[5] The use that Paul and later Christian writers made of traditional letter elements is clarified by such balance between recognizing the usual contours and functions of letter elements and knowing how they function in a particular letter. If Philemon, for instance, seems to reflect the Hellenistic letter of recommendation type, study of Paul's modifications of the standard discloses his creative freedom

5. White, "The Structural Analysis of Philemon," p. 25.

in appropriating such forms to express his own unique perception of the new religion.

Formal and Generic Traits. Formal elements are often confused with "forms" per se—a confusion that probably came about because of the inclusive scope of early form-critical studies. Obviously "form" is an entity that can cause instant multiplication of definitions at the drop of a scholar's hat, but, especially in the period following 1910, the form critics (especially Martin Dibelius) often confused formal elements with form as such, or confused formal with stylistic elements. Much of the subsequent study of form criticism has had to focus upon attaining greater clarity of terms. Current projects in literary criticism (such as the Old Testament Form Criticism Project) are stimulating debate concerning the proper definitions to be adopted.[6]

Part of the confusion centers around insufficient definition of form and genre; while we still hear of "the gospel form" or "the epistolary form," these literary units are larger than the forms which they contain, and should properly be termed genres (or subgenres, given a longer-range view of literary production in Hellenism). Genre refers to a particular patterning of materials common to a group of works—which are partly constituted by "forms." We may say that traits of a particular genre are the use of particular forms, as when we note that Hellenistic letters frequently utilize greeting—or thanksgiving—forms. Criticism by genres means identifying particular literary traits coalescing in particular patterns; it functions to identify incidental relationships to other works in the same type of literature and to call attention to lines of contact with similar traditional series.[7]

Our understanding of a work should therefore be organized somewhat as follows: the largest category we take to be the genre, as "the epistolary genre." Within the genre are various stylistic traits, characteristic forms, and recurring types. We have discussed the types of Hellenistic epistles in chapter one, and some generic traits in both chapters one and two (communication between absent

---

6. My own agenda includes work on generic ontology and the definitions of biblical genres, and I am aware of work by Rolf Knierim, Martin Buss, and Norman Petersen on similar problems. See especially the programmatic questioning by Erhardt Güttgemanns, *Offene Fragen zur Formgeschichte des Evangeliums,* 2nd ed. (Munich: Chr. Kaiser Verlag, 1971).

7. Northrup Frye, *Anatomy of Criticism* (Princeton: Princeton University Press, 1971), pp. 247–48; E. San Juan, Jr., "Notes Toward a Classification of Organizing Principles," *Genre* 1 (1968): 262.

friends; formal organization of the letter to reflect a substitute for oral encounter; use of stereotyped, recurring phrases). The criticism of any particular text must distinguish between the way in which a specific item—the greeting, for example—functions as a generic trait (a formal necessity that would cause consternation if it were omitted), or as a stylistic trait, as when Paul modifies the greeting to communicate his sense of authority and shared participation in Christian beginnings. Report on one's situation or response to news of the addressees can function as a generic trait having formal contours, or as the stylistic characteristic of a particular writer who uses the form to convey information in a previously agreed-upon code. Whenever a standardized formula exists, we must pay careful attention when an individual modifies it for his own purposes.

Use of Traditional Materials. Finally, the use of traditional materials, including traditional forms and styles, indicates the importance of contexts temporally prior to the writing that have been influential. Recent New Testament analysis has focused upon the identification of liturgical, hymnic, and creedal materials from the rich diversity of early Christianity as they have been worked into the New Testament epistolary literature. Such materials were used for many different purposes; for example, Furnish shows how Paul used traditional materials in his paraenesis for the purposes of instruction, for supporting promises or warnings, for encouragement, and to illustrate or to exemplify ideas.[8] Especially Scripture, i.e., the sacred writings of Israel, was used to buttress Christian arguments, to provide typological explanations, to demonstrate theological points, and to establish continuity between Israel and Christianity (the "new Israel").

Again the main point to be made is that discrimination must be made between religious emphases of the materials that are taken over, and the ways the materials are used in New Testament texts. It is naive to expect that a new religion such as Christianity, rising as it did out of Graeco-Roman matrices, would produce an entirely new body of religious materials; our concerns must include the sensitive delineations of received materials from the ways they came to be interpreted, as well as attempts to distinguish what is truly new. Our pictures of Paul and the other early Christian writers gain lustre and depth when we are able to appreciate their abilities

8. Victor P. Furnish, *Theology and Ethics in Paul* (Nashville: Abingdon Press, 1968), pp. 79–80.

to use traditions, and to understand how difficult a process it was to garner the best from several religious traditions while still maintaining some sense of religious uniqueness and identity.

Specific units of materials can be identified; generally we may speak of subforms within the epistles, and it is to the exploration of such materials that we now turn. By and large these forms reflect the ongoing life of the Christian communities as they went about their teaching, worship, and common life; their inclusion in the New Testament letters demonstrates how intimately the letters are reflections of the community life rather than being created as intellectual exercises. The letters served practical needs above all, and they provide us with our primary sources for the historical development of the primitive church.

FORMAL ELEMENTS IN THE LETTERS

The main divisions of the Pauline letters were discussed in chapter two, where we also indicated some of the contours of subunits of the epistolary sections. Those subunits were the ones most important within the Pauline letters; discussion here is centered around elements which are not exclusively epistolary in nature (although they may be epistolary), and which are not particularly unique to the Pauline correspondence. The size limitations and the formal orientation of this book mean that the treatment here must be catalogue-like. For each item I have indicated: bibliography, important or particularly clear studies, description of the unit itself, and at least one example. The value of the treatment should be in the manner in which it stimulates research and study of the particular units.

Autobiography. Beda Rigaux, *Letters of St. Paul*, pp. 122–23; Jack T. Sanders, "Paul's 'Autobiographical' Statements in Galatians 1–2," *JBL* 85 (1966): 335–43.

Rigaux is primarily concerned to classify statements in which Paul makes assertions about himself. He distinguishes: (a) simple autobiographies (2 Cor. 7:5, Phil. 1:12 ff.); (b) apostolic autobiography, reflecting on his past career with or on behalf of the addressees (1 Thess. 2:1–12, 2 Cor. 1:8–10); (c) apologetic and polemic autobiography (1 Cor. 9, Gal. 1:11–2:14); (d) mystical autobiography (2 Cor. 12:1 ff.; cf. Eph. 3:1–13); and (e) use of the first person pronoun in such a way as to seem a type (Rom. 7:14–25—I find his examples of this type to be unclear).

Sanders moves beyond Rigaux's simple listing of types of materials to ask how the autobiographical passage in Galatians 1–4 actually functions in Paul's argument; he finds that there is a formality about the passage which can be compared with other Pauline materials (such as 1 Cor. 15:1, 3), and which suggests that the point of this autobiographical passage is less historical precision than historic elucidation of the importance which Paul attached to his role as apostle. The passage is more important as theology than as chronology.

Apocalyptic. William G. Doty, "Identifying Eschatological Language," *Continuum* 7 (1970): 546–61 and *Contemporary New Testament Interpretation* (Englewood Cliffs: Prentice-Hall, Inc., 1972), pp. 129–31; John G. Gager, Jr., "Functional Diversity in Paul's Use of End-Time Language," *JBL* 89 (1970): 325–37; Graydon F. Snyder, "The Literalization of the Apocalyptic Form in the New Testament Church," *Biblical Research* 14 (1969): 5–18; P. Vielhauer, in Hennecke-Schneemelcher, *New Testament Apocrypha*, ed. R. McL. Wilson (Philadelphia: Westminster Press, 1963), pp. 581–642; A. N. Wilder, "The Rhetoric of Ancient and Modern Apocalyptic," *Interpretation* 25 (1971): 436–53.

The problem with inclusion of "apocalyptic" in a section on epistolary forms is that the term is more often used to indicate content than form. It may be that the most we can do is to suggest that certain forms are apocalyptic, and hope eventually to have some efficient criteria for making formal identifications.[9]

Characteristics given in most studies have to do with reference to the Parousia, apostolic afflictions and trials, various concepts of resurrection, angels or evil spirits, cosmological turmoil, the New Jerusalem, and the final judgment. As I understand generic or subgeneric form criticism, we shall also have to deal with a variety of factors, such as how time is evaluated (the relative importance of the present moment vis-à-vis the future), the ways in which good and evil are explained as part of divine purposes, the conditions of the projected end period, and the agencies responsible for eschato-

9. In addition to the attempts in the *Continuum* article (part of a special issue on eschatology), I am attempting to work out such criteria in a sequel, "Apocalyptic Style in the New Testament." The characteristics dealt with here are more extensively outlined in my *Contemporary New Testament Interpretation*, pp. 129–31. Gager's article is a good example of the much-needed approach which starts fresh from the texts themselves.

logical events. Literary description will include discussion of imaginative language and conventional symbols, the influence of the apocalypse form itself, and the self-consciousness of being "apocalyptic" rather than "normally" theological. Doubtless specific apocalyptic forms may eventually be sufficiently identified: I suspect that these may include symbolic utterances, visions, blessings, wisdom sayings, farewell discourses, and "revelation" sequences. The major New Testament passages to be analyzed are 1 Thess. 4:13–5:11, 2 Thess. 1:5–10, 2:1–17, 1 Cor. 15:12–28, Jude, 2 Peter 2–3, the Apocalypse to John, the Synoptic Apocalypse, Hebrews 1–2, and the longer ending to Mark.

Catalogues and Lists. Burton S. Easton, "New Testament Ethical Lists," *JBL* 51 (1932): 1–12; Victor P. Furnish, *Theology and Ethics in Paul;* J. N. D. Kelly, *The Epistles of Peter and of Jude* (New York: Harper & Row, 1969); O. J. F. Seitz, "Lists, Ethical," *Interpreter's Dictionary of the Bible,* vol. 3 (1962), pp. 137–39; Heinz-Dietrich Wendland, *Ethik des Neuen Testaments* (Göttingen: Vandenhoeck & Ruprecht, 1970).

I have not cited the classical literature on catalogues of vices and virtues and rules for the household; the works cited can lead the reader into these works, and they are mostly in German.[10] The materials involved are some of the most stereotyped materials used by the primitive Christians; Paul utilized such materials although not to as great an extent as did the post-Pauline literature. The lists provide a good case for studies of the relationships of the early church to Stoic and other Hellenistic contexts, and most of the technical literature is centered around tracing such parallels.

Catalogues or lists of vices or virtues figure in the New Testament as means of describing the moral life; in every case the virtues or vices listed are not characteristics of the particular community addressed, but the lists were used to enumerate general problem situations. Lists of vices include: Rom. 1:29–31, 13:13, 1 Cor. 5:10–11,

10. E. Kamlah, *Die Form der katalogischen Paränese im Neuen Testament* (Tübingen: J. C. B. Mohr [Paul Siebeck], 1964); D. Schroeder, *Die Haustafeln des Neuen Testaments: Ihre Herkunft und ihr theologischer Sinn* (Hamburg, 1959); W. Schrage, *Die konkreten Einzelgebote in den paulinischen Paränese. Ein Beitrag zur neutestamentlichen Ethik* (Gütersloh, 1961); A. Vögtle, *Die Tugend- und Lasterkataloge im Neuen Testament: Exegetisch, religions- und formgeschichtlich untersucht* (Münster, 1936); K. Weidinger, *Die Haustafeln. Ein Stück urchristlicher Paränese* (Leipzig: J. C. Hinrichs, 1928); S. Wibbing, *Die Tugend- und Lasterkataloge im Neuen Testament und ihre Traditionsgeschichte unter besonderer Berücksichtigung der Qumrantexte* (Berlin: Töpelmann, 1959).

LETTERS IN PRIMITIVE CHRISTIANITY

6:9–10, 2 Cor. 6:14, Gal. 5:19–21, Col. 3:5–8, Eph. 4:31–32, 5:3–4, 1 Tim. 1:9–10, 6:4, 2 Tim. 3:2–4, 1 Pet. 4:3 (and Rev. 9:20–21, 21:8, 22:15, and Mark 7:21–22). Lists of virtues include: Gal. 5:22–23, 2 Cor. 6:6–7, Phil. 4:8, Col. 3:12–15, Eph. 6:14–17, 1 Tim. 3:2–3, 6:11, Titus 1:7–8, James 3:17, 2 Pet. 1:5–8 (and the Beatitudes). Two basic types of lists can be distinguished. The first type is descriptive, and its context usually leads to threats or condemnation or to a contrast with Christian believers (cf. Rom. 1:28–32 and 1 Cor. 6:9–11); the second type is basically paraenetic, with the lists preaching a moral code of behavior (cf. Col. 3:5–11 and Gal. 5:16–24). Pairings—a list of vices followed by a contrasting list of virtues —are a common literary feature (cf. 2 Cor. 6). The listing of virtues may be followed by advice as to how they are to be manifested for particular ecclesiastical offices; they especially tend to be Christianized, i.e., taken up from their original framework and surrounded by Christian preaching.

Most scholars agree that the sociological setting for the use of these materials is the baptismal instruction; this setting, in addition to the (possible) Iranian dualistic background of such materials, may account for their extremely sharp contrasts between good and evil behavior.[11]

An additional type of catalogue, the catalogue of circumstances (*peristasis*) is found in reflections on apostolic careers, as seen in 2 Cor. 11:23–28 and 12:10.

Rules for the household (traditionally identified as *Haustafeln*, due to the influence of a heading in Luther's translation of the Bible) specify domestic duties and are another form of early Christian paraenesis. Such lists of rules are assimilated from Hellenistic contexts, and their use in primitive Christian contexts (Col. 3:18–4:1, Eph. 5:21–6:9, Titus 2:1–10) probably reflects a development of great importance for the primitive church: the turning away from asceticism to full engagement with the social and economic contours of secular life.[12] While the tables of rules may bear eschatological sentiments (especially emphasized by Hans Conzelmann), their importance was found in delineating day-to-day behavior.

11. Eduard Lohse, *Colossians and Philemon*, trans. W. R. Poehlmann and R. J. Harris, ed. H. Koester (Philadelphia: Fortress Press, 1971), pp. 137, 140 n. 37, calls attention to the 5 + 5 schema of the Colossians catalogue, and suggests that underlying it is an Iranian schema which had become traditional throughout the Hellenistic world, with parallels also at Qumran.
12. Wendland, *Ethik des Neuen Testaments*, pp. 46, 93 ff., 99.

Probably stressed mainly during baptismal or catechetical instruction, they are a good example of the adoption of non-Christian materials by the early church.

Additional "tables" of rules were formulated for guiding behavior within the primitive Christian religious communities (*Gemeindetafeln*): 1 Tim. 2:1–15, 5:1–21, 6:1–2, 2 Pet. 2:13–3:7. These emphasize how believers are to comport themselves toward non-Christians, and also concern the development of church administration and order (cf. 1 Tim. 3:4, 15). The form is well established by the post-Pauline letters, and is often represented in the Apostolic Fathers (Didache 4:9–11, Barnabas 19:5–7, 1 Clement 21:6–9, Polycarp to the Philippians 4:2–6:3).

Catechesis. Philip Carrington, *The Primitive Christian Catechism* (Cambridge, 1940); Edward Gordon Selwyn, *The First Epistle of St. Peter* (London: Macmillan & Co., 1946), pp. 363–466.

A common catechetical pattern in 1 Thess. 4:1–9 and 1 Pet. 1:13–22 is identified by Carrington and Selwyn, who describe the material as forming an early Christian holiness code, both by analogy with the Holiness Code of the Torah, and because the elements seem to be structured on the basis of reference to Leviticus 17–20. Common elements include stress upon the holiness of the Christian life, upon abstaining from immorality, and upon peace and brotherly love in the community. A second such pattern is found in 1 Pet. 2:1–2, James 1:21, Col. 3:8–4:12, Eph. 4:22 ff. It is identified by certain characteristic phrases: "put off" evil, "put on" the new Christian life-style, "be subject" to worthy authority, and "stand" fast in the sacred traditions of the church.

Such teaching was often introduced by appeals to common oral traditions and teachings ("we all know that . . ."). The presence of a formulary catechesis in 1 Thessalonians shows the early date at which such patterns were established. Carrington's suggestions that such materials can be specifically tied to connections with baptismal training has been supplemented by Selwyn; while it may not be feasible to identify passages as baptismal material as such, association with preparation for full participation in the Christian communities is certain, and the thought-complex surrounding baptism (contrast between light and darkness, contrasts between the old and the new life) must be kept in mind as framing these materials. The period of training and religious education before full membership was often a lengthy one in the early church, and it provided occasion for extensive training around such images.

Confessional Formulae. Vernon H. Neufeld, *The Earliest Christian Confessions* (Leiden: E. J. Brill, 1963). See this book for further bibliography.

The development of brief honorific titles for confessing faith in Jesus as God's agent is one of the most obscure aspects of primitive Christian history and theology. New Testament scholarship might be chronicled as the changing perspectives on such formulae. Discussion of christological formulae is not possible here, and so our attention must be upon the larger units of materials.

The profession of belief is of major significance for understanding the development of a religious community, for, as Neufeld notes, ". . . the *homologia* [confession] represented the agreement or consensus in which the Christian community was united, that core of essential conviction and belief to which Christians subscribed and openly testified."[13] The confession functions as an abbreviated statement of complex beliefs, as an outline of theology to be comprehended by the person joining the community, and as a symbol of shared perceptions by members of the community, especially in situations of corporate participation such as worship. It functions further as an important criterion of differentiation from competing religious groups, as a standard defense against oppressors or deviants, and as the theoretical basis for development of ethical and apologetic teaching.

Identification of confessional materials used in the letters follows criteria established by the work of several scholars, notably Ethelbert Stauffer and Oscar Cullmann. Literary characteristics such as the following are clues: the language of the immediate context of the statement may indicate, especially by the terms "deliver," "believe," or "confess," the presence of confessional materials (cf. Rom. 10:9, "if you confess with your lips that Jesus is Lord and *believe* in your heart that God raised him from the dead, you will be saved," and 1 Cor. 15:3 ff.); textual dislocation may point to such material (cf. 1 Tim. 3:16, "Great indeed—*we confess*—is the mystery of our religion . . ."); syntactical awkwardness, indicating borrowed materials (cf. Rev. 1:4, "Grace to you and peace from him *who is and who was and who is to come* . . ."); linguistic evidence may indicate

13. Neufeld, *The Earliest Christian Confessions*, p. 20.

terminological peculiarities (the Aramaic phrase *Marana tha*—O Lord come) or unique stylistic usage (cf. 1 Cor. 11:23, ". . . I also delivered to you, that *the Lord Jesus* . . ."); syntactical plainness may be one clue, since terse, "loaded" sentence fragments are typical; and finally, rhythmical or strophic composition may indicate the presence of confessional materials (when it does not indicate poetic or hymnic materials).

Hymnic Materials. Ralph P. Martin, "Aspects of Worship in the New Testament Church," *Vox Evangelica* (London: The Epworth Press, 1963), vol. 2, pp. 6–32; Gottfried Schille, *Frühchristliche Hymnen* (Berlin: Evangelische Verlagsanstalt, 1965); Rigaux, *Letters of St. Paul*, pp. 134–43.

The discussion concerning hymnic elements in the epistles, especially materials in Philippians and Colossians, has become too extensive to summarize adequately. A tentative list of passages treated as hymnic by various scholars can be made, with the reservation that identification of precise hymnic boundaries or definite hymnic structure for any particular passage is often hotly disputed by critics. The categories often overlap, reflecting the considerable methodological unclarity at the present time.

Sacramental—Baptismal and Eucharistic: Eph. 2:19–22 (14–18?), 5:14 ("Awake, O sleeper, and arise from the dead, and Christ shall give you light"); Titus 3:4–7; Rom. 6:1–11(?); Col. 2:9–15.

Initiation Hymns: Eph. 2:4–10; Rom. 3:23–25; Titus 2:11–14, 3:3–7; 2 Tim. 1:9–10 (Eph. 1:3–12, Col. 1:12–20).

Confessional: 1 Tim. 6:11–16; 2 Tim. 2:11–13; Col. 3:16; Eph. 5:19; Heb. 13:15.

Christ Hymns: Heb. 1:2–4, 5:5, 7:1–3; Col. 1:15–20; Phil. 2:6–11; 1 Pet. 1:18–20, 2:21–24, 3:18–22; 1 Tim. 3:16.

Hymnlike Meditations: Eph. 1:3–14; Rom. 8:31–39; 1 Cor. 13 (12:31–14:1?).

Scriptural Centos: Rom. 9:33, 1 Pet. 2:6–7.

Means of identifying hymnic and liturgical materials are similar to those used for identifying confessional materials; in addition to those listed above: hymnlike passages are frequently opened by a relative clause and continued by participles; rhythmical quality is pronounced; conscious parallelism or other grammatical features may be present; rare terms or terms unique to an author in this particular passage may produce an elevated style; introductory formulae may be used (Eph. 5:14, "Therefore it is said, . . ."); concluding statements may summarize the point of the quotation; and part of the contents of the passage may be extraneous to the reasons why the material has been inserted.

It is too early to speak confidently of form laws of early Christian hymnody and hymnic passages with confessional and other purposes; at best we are able to identify passages such as those listed here as bearing important links to the preliterary stages of New Testament texts, and caution must replace confidence in their interpretation.[14]

Judgment. Calvin Roetzel, "The Judgment Form in Paul's Letters," *JBL* 88 (1969): 305–12.

In the paraenetic section in two Pauline letters (1 Thess. 4:3–8, Gal. 6:7–10, 5:18–26), and in other sections of other letters (1 Cor. 3:16–17, 5:1–13, 10:1–14, 11:17–34; Rom. 1:18–32; 2 Thess. 1:5–12, 2:1–8, 9–15; and Gal. 1:6–9), Roetzel identifies a formulaic element having four features: (a) an introduction, (b) statement of an offense, (c) punishment threatened correlative to the offense, and (d) hortatory conclusion. The sequence of features may vary; a brief example from 2 Thess. 2:9–15: (a) The coming of the lawless one . . . with power; (b) and with deception; (c) God sends upon them delusion; (d) so stand firm to the traditions. In these statements Paul appears as the leader concerned with the church communities under his jurisdiction, and relates judgment to morality in a way reminiscent of the prophets of Israel. While Roetzel has successfully demonstrated the formulaic nature of the units, I suspect that the form is a weak one: it would be difficult to phrase statements of such content in any particular way. The subform may best be thought of as the result of Paul's experience in dealing with the particular issues (immorality, corruption, evil, ungodliness), especially since parallels in contemporary religious literature are not found.

Additional Formal Elements.

The survey of formal elements in the letters should indicate that form-critical analysis of the letters has begun—it should also indicate

---

14. Compare Edgar Krentz, "The Early Dark Ages of the Church—Some Reflections," *Concordia Theological Monthly* 41 (1970): 84: "It is a striking fact that no early Christian made a collection of these hymns and creeds. There was no tendency to standardization. Most formulas were saved by accident, by chance citation in paraenetic contexts. This ought to be enough to warn against overly hasty generalizations."

the preliminary nature of such study, and the need for sustained attention in the immediate future. Needing special attention are the following: liturgical materials,[15] specific items such as the rejoicing phrase (which may functionally replace the thanksgiving), the intercessory and petitionary phrases, exegetical patterns and scriptural-quotation formulae, and "kerygmatic" materials from pre-Pauline tradition.

15. Ernst Käsemann, "Formeln. II. Liturgische Formeln im NT," *Die Religion in Geschichte und Gegenwart*, 3rd. ed., vol. II (Tübingen, J. C. B. Mohr [Paul Siebeck], 1958), 993–96, and E. Hertzsch, "Liturgik. IV. Liturgische Formeln," ibid., vol. IV (1960), 423, list the following as liturgical formulae: acclamations (amen, alleluia); independent liturgical and sacramental formulae; doxologies; confessions; salutations; benedictions; blessings and curses; and predications of God. An adequately comprehensive treatment of all these materials is yet to be published. See also G. W. H. Lampe, "The Evidence in the New Testament for Early Creeds, Catechisms, and Liturgy," *Expository Times* 71 (1959–60): 359–63 for bibliography.

IV

Early Christian Letters

The importance of the fact that Paul wrote letters cannot be overestimated. He did not write gospels or apocalypses; he did not pass on his teaching in the form of grouped sayings or as parables, but in letters addressed to specific situations and local forms of Christianity. Paul, in spite of resistance during his life to his claim to be an apostle, attained apostolic status soon after his death. Finally, those among Paul's followers who thought that they especially understood what Paul had been up to came to feel that they could anticipate what Paul would have had to say to particular later situations. All of these factors explain the literature which arose after the time of Paul that was couched in his name—and in letters.

What better way to stress continuity with Paul than to form one's material into letters? And since standards of authorship were hardly as legalized and copyrighted as they are today, why not take the final step of claiming that the letters were from the hand of Paul? This is precisely what did happen, and of the twenty-one New Testament "letters," fourteen are thought by most New Testament scholars to come from the hands of writers later than Paul. The first group, the Deutero-Pauline letters, makes explicit claim to be Pauline, and includes the letters to Timothy and to Titus. These three together are usually termed the Pastoral letters; another group of writings does not claim to stem from Paul, but continues the use of the epistolary model—the so-called (since the fourth century) Catholic letters, the letters of James, Peter, and Jude, and the group is sometimes expanded to include Hebrews and the Johannine letters.

The Deutero-Pauline letters not only ape Paul's diction and his style of writing as one with authority, they also rather closely copy the Pauline letter form. Indeed the letters are so structured that the

Pauline form itself can be clarified by studying the formal organization of these letters, and one cannot argue for or against Pauline authorship solely on the basis of adherence to "Pauline form."[1] The whole question of Pauline influence upon the literature that was produced after his life is a difficult one; studies have tended to concentrate either upon the continuing influence of Pauline theological ideas or upon echoes of Pauline literary form, rather than upon the needed holistic approach which would seek a total picture of influences in form, ideas, structure, and sociological setting and function.

One of the most detailed studies of Pauline influence is by Alfred E. Barnett,[2] who identifies three periods of influence. During the first stage, the letters of Paul enjoyed great popularity (caused, according to the argument of Goodspeed, by the publication of Luke–Acts); a strong influence of the letters is demonstrated in Ephesians, Apocalypse to John, 1 Peter, Hebrews, Gospel of John, 1 Clement, Johannine Epistles, Ignatius, Polycarp. (Barnett's suggestions are seldom unanimously accepted for these materials.) A second period represents a subsidence of popularity of the letters occasioned by the frequent use of the letters by heretics; less influence, therefore, is found in James, Jude, Hermas, Barnabas, Didache, 2 Clement, The Martyrdom of Polycarp. And finally, in the second half of the second century, the letters became popular once again—as signified by their incorporation into the official canon of scripture. In this period 2 Peter, Justin, and the Pastoral letters show the growing influence of Pauline materials.

Difficulties with such attempts to trace influence abound. Future studies will have to go beyond Barnett's mainly theological analysis, and deal more carefully with formal matters as well as theological matters. We already see that attempts of this nature cannot be restricted to *Pauline* influence upon post-Pauline writings, but must include analysis of other influences as well.[3] It is also important to

1. Not all aspects of the Pauline form are copied: Paul Schubert, *Form and Function of the Pauline Thanksgivings*, Beihefte zur Zeitschrift für die Neutestamentliche Wissenschaft 20 (Berlin: Alfred Töpelmann, 1939), p. 9, notes that there are "only sporadic and fragmentary imitations of the Pauline thanksgivings." Blessings, however, develop all the more strongly.

2. Albert E. Barnett, *Paul Becomes a Literary Influence* (Chicago: University of Chicago Press, 1941); supplementing the old standard, Oxford Society of Historical Theology, *The New Testament in the Apostolic Fathers* (Oxford: Clarendon Press, 1905; 2nd ed., 1921).

3. See especially Carl Andresen, "Zum Formular frühchristlicher Gemeindebriefe," *Zeitschrift für die Neutestamentliche Wissenschaft* 56 (1965): 233–59.

remember that lack of quotation or explicit use of Pauline materials may not indicate lack of "Pauline influence." The post-Pauline materials were often directed to situations (e.g., to apologetics or to combatting heresies), for which Paul's arguments against the Judaizers did not supply much support directly, although the author might otherwise be greatly influenced by Pauline thought.

General comparative features of the post-Pauline letters are as follows:

1. *Type.* The basic type of letter established by Paul is continued. The letters are means of continuing a religious movement, especially shaping and regulating its activity. At least by conscious fiction a major apostolic writer extends information across physical distance to a person or a community.

2. *Ecclesial Letters.* At the same time, however, there is development of the Christian letter tradition: the Pastoral, then the Catholic, letters show that the Pauline letter was being developed in the direction of the later official churchly epistolary writings (the encyclical, the episcopal or synodal letters—writings sent out in letter form which expressed the decisions of church conferences or ecclesiastical administrators). If the uniqueness of the Pauline letter is the intensity with which Paul was directly involved in each epistolary situation, referring to specific troublemakers or problems within the Christian communities he founded, what is characteristic of the post-Pauline letters (not just the Catholic letters!) is precisely their generality, their catholicity. Specific individuals are still mentioned, but because of their danger to the church catholic; there is a church-consciousness present which could not have been a possibility in Paul's lifetime. Soon—since copies of Paul's letters were to be found throughout primitive Christianity (although not necessarily the entire corpus at any one location)—Paul's letters came to be understood as having been as catholic and general in intent as were the post-Pauline writings.

3. *Authorship.* Since Paul came to be considered the role model for those in authority over dispersed church communities, his model as a letter writer was similarly copied. Identification with Paul went to the extent that later authors felt that they were extending Paul's own work. Hence there was nothing strange about actually writing in Paul's name,[4] or in the name of another apostolic leader.

---

4. Cf. Hans Lietzmann, *A History of the Early Church*, trans. B. L. Woolf (Cleveland: The World Publishing Company, 1961), vol. 1, p. 193: "Feeling himself to be the heir of Paul, (Clement) shows clearly both in his words of

4. *Literary Works.* We are also well along the trajectory of the early Christian letter when we realize that the post-Pauline letters do not display the sense of dialogic participation that is found in Paul's writings. We may be able to identify some of the opponents in the post-Pauline letters, but we do not often sense that they are replies to other letters. If Paul wrote only reluctantly, or at any rate made provision for augmenting his written word with his oral confrontation or by the message entrusted to the messenger, it is characteristic of the post-Pauline writings that they are *literary* creations in their own right, and do not presuppose supplementation by an oral or another written message.[5]

5. *Traditional Teachings.* The catholicity of these works, and their self-conscious literary quality is reinforced by a great regard for the successful traditional teachings of early Christianity that have now accumulated. The Pastoral letters, while constituted externally as specific admonitions to Timothy and Titus, are actually guide books for the offices of ecclesiastical leadership in Christian churches everywhere (bishops, deacons: 1 Timothy 3; teachers and preachers: 1 Timothy 4, 6; 2 Timothy 2–4, Titus; elders: 1 Timothy 5; and prophets). Hebrews reflects on "these last days" in general (1:2); the Catholic letters show the generalizing trend in their openings ("to the twelve tribes in the dispersion," James 1:1, even "to those who are called," Jude 1); and the Johannine letters, especially the first one, deal with the explication of Christian love in ways which are hardly exhausted by their attempts to deal with problems of gnosticism.

6. *Treatise Form.* Several of the letters go beyond the Pauline letters, which retain their ties to the Greek private letter structure, to attain letter-essay form. This is especially true of Hebrews, which has only an epistolary opening, and 1 John.[6] The Pauline letters may

greeting, and in the whole style of his introduction, that he intended to write a letter in the way the Apostle was accustomed to write to his churches when in need of earnest exhortation. It feels almost like this: if Clement had not been commissioned by the Roman church, but had written on his own initiative, he would probably have written the author's name as 'Paul, the apostle of Jesus Christ,' and we should have possessed another pseudo-Pauline letter." Pseudonymous authorship in Hellenism was briefly discussed in chapter one.

5. Cf. Johannes Sykutris, "Epistolographie," *Real-Encyclopädie der classischen Altertumswissenschaft,* Suppl. vol. 5 (1931), p. 219: "For Paul the letter grows out of immediate reality, out of the necessity of the moment. For Paul's followers the form is utilized in abstraction from such reality as a form of literature."

6. Hebrews seems to be patterned by continual alteration of paraenesis and

be understood as the first and last pure type of the ecclesial (churchly) genre, with developments toward letter-essays as the subsequent adaptation and modification of that genre; or as far as extensiveness in time is concerned, we could suggest that the pure genre is reached in the later, ecclesial, letter-essay form, and that the Pauline letters are the pre-complete stage of the generic development. (We ought not assume that the Pauline letter has to be the model type—an assumption easily made because of Paul's *theological* importance.)

THE PSEUDO-PAULINE AND UNIVERSAL LETTERS

Ephesians and Colossians have so many ties to the Pauline letters that they have frequently been understood as stemming from Paul himself. While defenders of Pauline authenticity can still be found— especially for Colossians—both letters are usually considered today to come from followers of Paul, who were familiar with his language, form, and theology. Ephesians, because it seems to summarize and draw together Pauline thought (especially on the nature of the church), has been considered as a brief introduction to the letters of Paul. More likely it is an attempt to present a summary, together with post-Pauline developments of theology, based on but superseding Paul. Fortunately it was not so successful that it led to suppression of the original letters!

Colossians similarly reflects Pauline imagery, theology, and letter form, although there are clear differences in theological understanding. Second Thessalonians also reflects very close ties to Paul, but its differences are such that it may also be best described as originating from a developing "Pauline school" rather than from the hand of Paul; the writing may have been occasioned primarily by attempts to modify Pauline eschatology. Ephesians, Colossians, and 2 Thessalonians are often grouped as the "Pseudo-Pauline letters."

The Pastoral (or "Deutero-Pauline") letters portray the clearest examples of the attempt to rest on Paul's laurels, while making "Paul" say what their author(s?) thought Paul would have said if he had been alive to confront the situations of their own later times. I find it to be characteristic of these letters that the Pauline paraenetic section is now lost to view formally: the letters are thoroughly permeated with the sort of advice and instruction which Paul usu-

---

sermon; but there may be an influence of epistolary style in the conclusion: paraenesis, 13:1–19; concluding benediction, 13:20–21; and final "personal" word with greetings and a wooden travelogue, 13:22–25.

ally treated in the fourth part of his letters. Similarity to the Pauline letters, however, is especially pronounced with respect to the epistolary situation—the Pastoral letters are concerned with immediate problems confronting the churches, especially deviant theologies, rather than with generalized dogma. In fact, generalized dogma has already been established, and these letters assume its defense and care to be their main purpose. Such purpose is mainly manifested, however, in concerns for developing ecclesiastical structures and officials.

The Universal ("Catholic") letters portray the furthest remove from the casual private letters of Hellenism. The letter form has become establishment form, and discernible influences stem more from self-consciously literary tracts and open letters than from the Pauline letters. The Letter of James, for instance, has only the opening of the letter form, used to introduce a collection of moral maxims and exhortations. James probably represents the culmination of the process of anthologizing moral teachings begun in the early lists and catalogues discussed in chapter three. As with those lists, pre- or non-Christian precursors may be suggested: James is sometimes referred to as a Christianized Jewish tract on morals. At any rate, letter form is not an important structural characteristic.

First and Second Peter and Jude repeat epistolary conventions to a greater extent, but it is difficult to conceive of these writings as having originated from actual epistolary contexts. Our knowledge of usual epistolary form no longer guides us through a sequence of units, all interrelated and mutually supportive. Rather, these writings are best understood as tracts expressing support for those undergoing persecution for their religion—persecution both from the state and from deviant Christians. Theological reflections now revolve around the sacred Christian traditions, not around the necessary shaping of the religion in specific contexts. We are not far from the idealized picture of one unitary religion expressed throughout the Christian world, as presented by Eusebius.

The first "letter" of John has completely lost epistolary characteristics, and it is doubtful that it would be called a letter if it had been transmitted apart from 2 and 3 John, which do appear in epistolary form. In fact 2 and 3 John are very much exceptions to the movement away from real letters: they correspond to a greater extent than the Pauline letters with Greek common letter traditions.[7]

7. Robert W. Funk, "The Form and Structure of II and III John," *JBL* 86 (1967): 424–30.

The seven letter corpus which opens the Apocalypse to John is the creation of its author, the number of letters being determined by the inner logic of the Apocalypse rather than by imitation of the specific number of epistles in the Pauline corpus. The letters are brief symbolic writings, to be understood on the basis of the context of end-time revelation; rather than as having recourse to previous letters.

The two letters in the second volume of Luke's work (Acts 15: 23b–29, 23:26–30) are, like the speeches in Acts, the product of the author of the two-volume work. The first of the two letters may reflect the custom of sending letters between the primitive Christian communities, especially when particular persons were delegated as official representatives. The second letter is supposed to be the letter concerning Paul sent by Claudius Lysias to Felix.

POST-CANONICAL LETTERS

Given the popularity of the epistolary form, it is striking that there are very few apocryphal letters.[8] The apocryphal epistles we do have are on the whole occasioned by references within the Pauline corpus: the Epistle to the Laodiceans, similar to Philippians in content, seeks to supply the missing letter of Col. 4:16 (". . . and see that you read also the letter from Laodicea"—the epistle itself ends v. 20: ". . . and see to it that this letter is read to the Colossians and their letter to you."). The Muratorian Fragment lists a further Epistle to the Alexandrians which, it says, was "forged in Paul's name for the sect of Marcion," and is not fit to be "received in the catholic church." A Third Epistle to the Corinthians is contained in the apocryphal Acts of Paul and is supposedly an answer to a letter sent by the Corinthians to Paul.

The most famous of the apocryphal Pauline epistles is the collection of eight letters from Seneca to Paul, together with Paul's six short replies (Correspondence between Paul and Seneca). Written in Latin in the third century, the correspondence was intended as a means of encouraging reading of Paul's epistles in social circles where their low literary style had been offensive.

8. Apocryphal materials are those writings from the first centuries of Christian literature which are not included in the New Testament canon, or in the Apostolic Fathers. Gnostic materials that are technically "apocryphal" are not usually included in the standard collections. The texts of the apocryphal letters are best studied in Hennecke-Schneemelcher, *New Testament Apocrypha,* ed. R. McL. Wilson (Philadelphia: Westminster Press, 1963); see also Johannes Quasten, *Patrology* (Utrecht: Spectrum Publishers, 1962), vol. 1.

A writing transmitted as the Epistle of Titus, a disciple of Paul, is not a letter but a fifth-century Latin address on virginity related to the writings of Pseudo-Cyprian. The first part of the Kerygmata Petrou, the so-called Epistle of Peter, takes the form of a letter of transmission from Peter to James; an apocryphal letter of Pontius Pilate to Claudius is to be found in the late Acts of Peter and Paul. A Syriac version exists of the correspondence between Jesus and King Abgar of Edessa which is mentioned by Eusebius; this document enjoyed great popularity in the fourth and fifth centuries as a text for protective amulets and hence it is frequently found in Christian papyri.

And finally, the anti-gnostic Epistle of the Apostles of the second century has the form of an apocalypse rather than the form of a letter. Its title came from the first paragraph where the conversations between Jesus and his apostles were identified as "what Jesus Christ revealed to his disciples as a letter."

Given these few examples of apocryphal letters in contrast to the great amount of other apocryphal materials, we may note that the letter form of the New Testament literature is not continued to any extent in the apocryphal New Testament. The apocryphal "letters" are mainly: (a) theological tracts in letter-form (Laodiceans, 3 Corinthians), (b) imaginative literary attempts (Epistle of the Apostles), (c) materials seeking to establish "proofs" (Pilate literature, the Epistle of Peter), or (d) literary propaganda (Paul and Seneca). Whatever the reason,[9] the epistolary form is not important in the preserved apocryphal materials; but it is striking in the "Apostolic Fathers," and it is to this group of early Christian writers that we now turn.

Outside the New Testament, the earliest Christian writing for which we have historical attestation of the name, date, and position of the author is an anonymous "letter" to the church at Corinth. The document, written about 96 C.E., is ascribed in later manuscripts to Clement, and has received the title, 1 Clement. Occasioned by a schism within the Corinthian church (". . . because of one or two

---

9. M. R. James, *The Apocryphal New Testament* (Oxford: Clarendon Press, 1924), p. 476, suggests that epistles were too difficult to forge; W. Michaelis, *Die Apokryphen Schriften zum Neuen Testament*, 2nd ed. (Bremen: Carl Schünemann, 1958), p. 440, that the letter form was not extensive enough to carry the intended content; Schneemelcher, in Hennecke-Schneemelcher, *New Testament Apocrypha*, vol. 2, p. 90, agrees that the form could not bear the purposes of the apocryphal writers, which was the "proclamation of the gospel." Such suggestions presuppose a distinction between the generic nature of gospel and letter which seems to me to be inadequate.

individuals the solid and ancient Corinthian Church is in revolt against its presbyters," 47:6), the writing draws upon the authority of the apostles, Holy Scripture, the examples of the saints, and finally "the letter of the blessed Apostle Paul" (47:2) to project means of restoring and maintaining the love which "knows nothing of schism or revolt" (49:5) in Christian communities.[10]

It is in the letters of Ignatius that we find the clearest reflections of Pauline letters; Ignatius evidently knew the Pauline corpus quite well, as he quotes frequently from 1 Corinthians, as well as from most of the other letters. His freedom toward the Pauline materials however is also marked: in the letter to the Trallians, a non-Christian greeting is used alongside a hearty greeting which claims to be "in the apostolic manner." As in the Pauline letters, Ignatius's letters are addressed to specific Christian communities, and frequently utilize reference to a particular problem to describe patterns of Christian behavior.[11]

The bishop of Smyrna, Polycarp, sent a collection of Ignatius's letters to the Philippian church, and used the occasion to send along a letter dealing with the problem of the behavior of church officials (especially of the presbyter Valens). Although Polycarp, the author of this letter to the Philippians, is not "well versed in the sacred scriptures" (as the Philippians are said to be, 12:1), his letter is a veritable mosaic of quotations and allusions to writings in the New Testament canon. Using Paul's letters especially, the epistle itself is a curious blend of occasional writing (concerning the Ignatian letters and questions of conduct) and of treatiselike exhortation.

Polycarp was martyred in 156, and the account of his martyrdom, The Martyrdom of Polycarp, was written the following year. Set in the form of a letter from "The church of God that sojourns at Smyrna to the church of God that sojourns at Philomelium, and to all those of the holy and Catholic Church who sojourn in every place" (introduction), the writing is most closely related to the Hellenistic public letter in occasion and form.

"A theological tract and a letter only in appearance" is the way

10. A so-called Second Epistle of Clement is not a letter at all but a sermonic writing, anonymous, and from a time before 150 c.e. Two letters *De virginitate* are ascribed to Clement of Rome also, but come from the third century.

11. Spurious letters of Ignatius exist; see especially Milton F. Brown, *The Authentic Writings of St. Ignatius* (Durham: Duke University Press, 1963), which is a contribution to the use of linguistic and stylistic criteria in determining authorship of manuscripts from antiquity.

Johannes Quasten describes the Epistle of Barnabas.[12] This second-century writing lacks any reference to specific situations, and falls into dogmatic (1–17) and moralistic (18–21) parts. Emphasizing the Old Testament, Barnabas also shares the Didache's emphasis upon the ethical theme of the Two Ways.[13]

We have no letters preserved from the Greek Apologists except for the Epistle to Diognetus (discussed in the next paragraph). The lack of letters is best explained by the literary nature of the attacks made upon Christianity by representatives of classical traditions such as the satirist Lucian, by Marcus Aurelius's teacher Fronto, or by the Platonist Celsus. Such opponents put forth rhetorical and dialectical attacks against Christianity, and the apologists responded in literary kind: in dialectic, dialogues, or, like Justin, in true apology style ("Against . . .", or "On . . .").

Nothing is known of the author or the addressee of the third-century Epistle to Diognetus, which is an apology for Christianity composed in letter form. The almost classical literary style of the epistle and its Pauline and Johannine overtones combine to give us an apology of beauty and literary merit.

The epistolary form is not well represented in the beginnings of the heretical literature which has been preserved,[14] but the development of anti-heretical materials evidences wide use of epistolary form. These materials are represented especially in the papal and episcopal letters in the latter part of the second and the first part of the third centuries (Pope Soter, Eleutherus). Letters were also the main medium of expression for practical problems (the date of Easter, Victor; letters by Dionysius, Serapion). Eusebius reports on several letters of Irenaeus.

Among the Alexandrian fathers, only Origen and Dionysius are represented; the extent of the materials is indicated by Jerome's citation of four different collections of Origen's letters. One of these

12. Quasten, *Patrology*, vol. 1, p. 85.

13. See Robert A. Kraft, *The Didache and Barnabas,* The Apostolic Fathers 3 (New York: Thomas Nelson & Sons, 1965).

14. We have fragments of one of Valentinus's letters, a letter by Ptolemy, and part of one by Marcion; from the recent Nag-Hammadi finds, the Epistle of Peter, one to Rheginos, the Epistle of the Blessed Eugnostus, and others. The literary genres of the Gnostic materials are currently under extensive debate. Malcolm Lee Peel, *The Epistle to Rheginos* (Philadelphia: Westminster Press, 1969), notes that Rheginos has been called variously "a treatise, a doctrinal letter, a letter, an epistle, a discourse, a tract, a pamphlet, and a book" (p. 6; cf. pp. 6–12).

comprised nine volumes, and was edited by Eusebius; of one hun-
dred letters in one of the volumes alone, we have only two com-
plete examples.

The Festal and the Papal letters of the third century are important not only for their picture of the Christianity of the day, but also
for the extent to which we can see how firmly ecclesiastical Latin
had been established. These letters dealt with all sorts of ecclesiastical matters: declaration of heresy, reconciliation of apostates, collections of money, consolations, and theological issues.

We can mention only in passing the important collections of letters from Cyprian, from Basil and Gregory Nazianzus. The progres-
sive development of the use of letters continues for generations,
reaching through the Middle Ages, and continuing in a formal sense
to this day, in the form of papal encyclicals and even "Ecumenical
Notes" from the World Council of Churches. A "golden age" was
reached, however, about 350–450, when rhetorical standards of the
Roman classical tradition were established in Christian epistolography. And in Byzantium we have the continuation of the tradition
to a high degree:

The letter belongs to the genres that were most eagerly and successfully
cared for within Byzantium. There is in this period hardly any literary
person of repute from whom we do not have a letter-collection.[15]

The fall of Constantinople and the flight of Byzantium's learned
men to the West meant only a hindering, not a cessation, of the
letter tradition.

INTERPRETIVE REFLECTIONS

Three factors seem most relevant as I review the trajectory of
early Christian letters: (a) the transition from oral to written modes
of expression, (b) the contextual and practical nature of the process
of theologizing that is reflected in letters, and (c) the early levels of
Christian religion that are present. These are discussed in sequence.

My own sense of the matter is that the Christian letters are less
to be understood as "almost oral" in nature than as direct reflections
of the very stage of development when primitive Christianity made
the important transition from oral to written modes of expression.
The development of widely dispersed centers of the religion and
the waning of the first generations made a written mode necessary;

15. Sykutris, "Epistolographie," p. 219.

the process was facilitated by the spread of the religion to educated and more financially gifted individuals. I suspect that all religions originate in an oral phrase—the phase when the originative inputs are being selected and emphasized. As far as Christianity is concerned, this period would encompass the work of Jesus and then those who first chose to stake their fortunes on his interpretations of Judaism, including Paul.

Writing became essential in order to organize the Jesus traditions and the witness to Jesus as God's agent (as "the Christ"). Collections of Jesus-materials seem indeed to represent the first preliterary stage of Christianity; the work of people like Paul would surely represent the second stage, since Paul could obviously not be everywhere at once, and found it necessary to communicate in some way. There is no reason to suppose that Paul's initial communications were not oral—we must be wary of conceiving of him as primarily a writer. He found it necessary to communicate in writing, however, and at some stage of his career began to write letters to accompany messengers and religious leaders whom he and others sent out. Paul may have continued to send oral information and instruction in instances where he did not send letters, as he surely did send additional instructions to the communities of Christians to whom he wrote letters.

So in the Pauline letters we are confronted with a writer who at best wrote unwillingly, and whose "natural" preference was to speak directly with those to whom circumstances forced him to address letters. Studies of Pauline theology ought to recognize the sense in which the materials in the letters are fragmentary with respect to their representation of the man as he would have been known by his contemporaries.

In the transition to written means of expression, Paul wrote in what must have been at best a temporary sense of literature: except for Romans, I doubt that Paul conceived of his letters surviving him by many years. (I understand Romans as at least partly Paul's final testament and summation of his solutions to problems of Christian theology.) It may be that other New Testament letters were as transitory in intent, but especially the later letters seem to have made the transition and to have become literature by conscious intent.

Instead of continuing as only a possible interpretation of Judaism, Christianity had now become an independent religion needing its own theological materials. The later letters reflect these needs and are especially oriented toward providing interpretations of Christian origins. The perspective of Luke—who understood Christianity as lasting for an indefinite period of time—was soon commonplace, and the post-Pauline epistolary literature functions more and more as the basis for preservation of religious positions attained rather than as the means of shaping new religious contours.

It may well be that contemporary theological reflection can learn from the primitive Christian letters that spirit of immediacy, creativity, and aliveness that characterized the earliest epistolary attempts. Christianity then was more tentative, less institutionalized, and more a matter of intense concentration upon possible new religious form and meaning than adoration of an establishment. One does not blithely turn one's back on the intervening centuries of Christian thought, and I am not advocating an ahistorical "back to primitivism." But surely contemporary Christianity can benefit from reflection on its originative dynamisms as it seeks to meet the cultural challenges of today which so resemble those of Hellenism. We may have to shed our sense of the New Testament epistles as "churchy" in order to appreciate their secular dynamics.

The second factor is closely related to the first. The materials in the letters are closer than we may ever penetrate otherwise to the founding language-events of primitive Christianity. In the letters we confront the linguistic newness and creativity of the primitive Christian movement as nowhere else. To the letters, then, we must turn for a sense of how that linguistic and religious newness was encountered. We are interested in the patterns of response to the tensions generated by the dynamism of the new religious movement, especially tensions arising from confrontations with the movement's cultural setting. We may no longer share the language of these earlier patterns, and because our contexts are so different from theirs, our responses will be quite different also. But the challenge to contemporary men is that they be as creative in responding to modern conditions as the primitive Christians were in responding to Graeco-Roman conditions.

And finally, the letters portray a religion which does not separate a sacred from a profane understanding of existence any more than it separates theology from economics. Its ethics is contextual, not in the sense that each context is a totally new challenge and that challenge must control the response, but insofar as previously learned guidelines remain guidelines and not dogmatic laws. Its literary models were not primarily the traditional religious ones we would

77

have expected. Jewish models were influential, but no more so than Hellenistic religious and secular models, and possibly not as influential. What came to be the New Testament was not only new in its appropriation of the Israelite theological heritage, but new in its adaptation of literary genres: the gospel genre as well as the ecclesial letters have analogues but not direct models.

We are confronted in the New Testament, in the words of Amos N. Wilder, "with a depth of mind, a sense of existence, which transcends our usual categories. These founders of Christianity were in the grip of over-mastering forces in a critical hour. . . . A great faith of this kind projects its own vision upon the world, it makes its own world, and employs a language proper to such experience,"[16] and the new language also led to new literary modes. If "the letter was the koine [common Greek] form of the koine language in the koine life . . .",[17] then the early Christian letter was uniquely the Christian form for the ongoing development of the Christian koine life, and letters supplement the other early Christian writings to present the most vivid picture of that religion taking shape and form.

The importance of tracing religious movements through the total cultural milieux in which they appear has been stressed recently in *Trajectories through Early Christianity*, by James M. Robinson and Helmut Koester.[18] We are going to have to give up the old standard presentations of Christianity which highlighted a simple religion centered on the Christ and keeping itself pure from external forces, in order to understand the real complexities and syncretisms of the primitive Christian movement.

A renewed approach to the historical development of the early church is becoming more prevalent and more clearly defined.[19] In few other fields has such a thoroughgoing rethinking of historiographic approaches taken place, and it seems possible that the next fifty years will witness the first truly comprehensive history of prim-

16. Amos N. Wilder, *New Testament Faith for Today* (London: SCM Press Ltd., 1956), p. 48.

17. M. Luther Stirewalt, Jr., "A Survey of the Uses of Letter-Writing in Hellenistic and Jewish Communities through the New Testament Period" (photocopy for the Society of Biblical Literature Seminar on the Form and Function of the Pauline Letters, 1971), p. 30.

18. James M. Robinson and Helmut Koester, *Trajectories through Early Christianity* (Philadelphia: Fortress Press, 1971).

19. I discuss this approach in "Emphasis upon the Historical: Recent Evaluations of Primitive Christianity," in *Contemporary New Testament Interpretation* (Englewood Cliffs: Prentice-Hall, Inc., 1972), pp. 89–104.

itive Christianity. It can only be completed if scholars will relinquish traditional fiefs in order to share cooperatively from their expertise in philosophy, sociology, linguistics, theology, history, and literary criticism. I would hope especially that the new approaches will remain as receptive to literary analysis as they are at the present time. We shall have to deal much more adequately with the development of generic trajectories if we are to integrate the study of the primitive Christian literature with the study of Hellenistic literature.

Epistles seem to have presented a unique genre for expression of the early growth of the churches; they were transformed into what was probably the most important literary genre of the early church, and our apperception of why this was so must go hand in hand with appreciation of the two other genres of the canon, the gospel and the history. Issues to be clarified include: Why was it that someone such as Paul wrote epistles rather than gospels? Why did the epistolary genre continue into the ecclesial letter genre, while the gospel genre effectively came to an end with the canonical gospels?[20] Can we conclude that there were ontological features of the epistolary genre that corresponded to the existential needs of the primitive Christians—needs not satisfied by the gospel or the history? What is the relation between gospels and letters in terms of their respective nearness to the founding events of the religion?

And, finally, our future explorations may find it possible to demonstrate more adequately the theological impulses of the primitive church which led its members to comprehend Christianity as a religion constantly in formation rather than as a religion characterized by recourse to solidified and frozen traditions of the past. That the later New Testament epistles have come to represent such a view may be linked to the wide promulgation and acceptance of the gospels, but the response of the early catholic church may not necessarily be demanded by the inner dynamics of Christianity as such, and contemporary appropriation of New Testament traditions need not be bound by the formula that the latest is necessarily the best.

Apart from the question of appropriation, however, there remain questions as to the relative linguistic effectiveness of the various primitive Christian literary types. A parallel contemporary question will clarify the point: given that many critics are convinced that the

20. The "gospels" in the New Testament apocrypha are a much more romantic type of literature than the New Testament gospels, and they portray greater influence of Hellenistic biographical models.

fictional novel has "died" as a viable contemporary genre, can we conclude that its "death" is a cultural phenomenon? That is, are novelists no longer able to engage meaningfully the complex levels of reality that confront us, must they, therefore, bow out before sociologists and psychologists? Questions of this sort lead us to ask about levels of language effectiveness.

I would argue that the epistle remained a viable and popular genre within early Christianity precisely because "it worked" to meet cultural needs. The epistle was just the form of language act necessary to the exploratory expansion of the primitive Christian movement. Letters of the Pauline sort did not function primarily to set out dogmas and locked-in theological criteria of faith. To be sure, these letters were not noncommittal! They certainly expressed Paul's position on important religious issues, and sometimes they were much too ethos-reflecting to suit our sophisticated tastes (Paul's low view of women, for example). But integral to the movement of the letters is a dialogic quality, a willingness to be addressed by the religious perspectives one was recalling. Paul felt that his whole career and self-identity rested upon whether or not his teaching was "from God," and hence whether it succeeded or not. For this reason he was so greedy for news from his churches, and also so concerned that the small "presence" which he might exert through his writings be reinforced by his actual personal presence.

When we look at the *post*-Pauline epistolary materials, there is less tentativeness, less dialogic tension, more confidence that the Christian religion had an important if not essential place in God's guidance of human affairs. And the epistle modulates away from its Pauline dialogic immediacy. I have tried to approach this without the common theological judgment that the Pauline writings are more important for Christian theology than the later New Testament writings, but as far as my appreciation of primary creativity is concerned, I come to a similar position. I have tried to indicate an openness to whatever part of the primitive Christian tradition "works best" for our own day. At any rate, the question of which materials are to be most appropriated becomes a religious question (the question of the canon within the canon), and the language critic can only hope to expose the contours and to suggest which materials are full of primary linguistic potency and which are secondary.

Books such as this one project some starting points, and are intended to provoke further reflection and refinement. We must learn much more about linguistic effectiveness and about generic criticism before we will be able to compare adequately the important differences between literary modes such as epistle, apocalypse, and gospel. Recent developments in linguistics, in structuralism, and in language-sociology and language-psychology demand prompt attention by the biblical critic, and seem to some of us to represent the most important new "inputs" into our field in recent years. It may well be—and I regard this as highly desirable—that biblical literary criticism will be deparochialized and reintegrated with nonreligious literary criticism in the future. Then we may approach genres such as the ecclesial epistle from the wide perspective of world literature and propose more confidently than we now can what made the primitive Christian literary types so effective for the Christian religion during its formative years.

Glossary

APOCALYPTIC—See Eschatology.

B.C.E., C.E.—Before the Common Era, Common Era—terms corresponding to the Christian B.C. and A.D.

BLESSING—Epistolary section which, in Christian use, replaced the thanksgiving; states the reason why gods are to be thanked or praised; influenced by liturgical language.

CATECHISM, CATECHETICAL—(Greek, *catechesis*) Moral and religious instruction in fundamental or elementary beliefs, as a condition for full membership in a religious community.

DIATRIBE—(Greek) A form of rhetoric used by Cynic and Stoic popular philosophers in street preaching; some of its conventions are reflected in New Testament letters.

ECCLESIAL—Arbitrary term to designate the adaptation of Graeco-Roman letters by the primitive Christian churches for purposes of ecclesiastical business, communications, and education.

EPISTOLARY, EPISTOLOGRAPHER—Adjective form of epistle, which is used synonymously with letter in this volume; one who writes epistles.

ESCHATOLOGY; APOCALYPTIC—Eschatology refers to self-conscious reflection about how the world will eventuate, especially with respect to divine purposes. Apocalyptic, a specific mode of eschatology, concerns specifically the dramatic incursion of the End into history, usually in elaborate figurative language and symbols.

HELLENISM, HELLENISTIC—The period in Greece, Rome, and the Near East from the time of Alexander's conquests (334–325 B.C.E.) to approximately the sixth century C.E. (after the "Hellenic" and before the "Byzantine" periods).

KERYGMA, KERYGMATIC—The apostolic "message" about Jesus the Christ; generally in preaching style.

LITURGY, LITURGICAL—The formalized pattern of worship; referring to materials derived from the contexts of religious cult and worship.

PAPYRUS (plural Papyri)—The predominant writing material throughout antiquity, made from the reedlike fibers of a river plant. Primarily used in single sheets. "The papyri" in this volume usually refers to letters transmitted on such materials—which were not long-lasting and were used for daily affairs.

PARAENESIS, PARAENETIC—Greek word for "advice." Ethical, edifying material, often associated with moral instruction or preaching.

PAROUSIA—Greek word for "presence." 1. Here mostly the reference is to presence, i.e., letters were a substitute form of being with another person; 2. the apostolic parousia: sections of Pauline letters where Paul indicates his intention to be with the addressees in the future; 3. technical use in primitive Christian theology: the presence ("second coming") of the Christ at the end of time.

PHARISAIC—Refers to the main tendency within postbiblical Judaism that became the backbone of the rabbinical movement toward the end of the first century C.E.

PHILOPHRONESIS, PHILOPHRONETIC—The "friendly feelings" which Greek letter theorists inculcated as essential to correspondence.

PSEUDONYMOUS—Used to designate writings when the true author is not known, although the writing does have an author's name attached by tradition; often an author wrote in the name of a recognized authority in order to lend support to his own views.

TALMUDIC—Pertaining to the codification of rabbinical traditions in the two Talmudim (Babylonian and Palestinian); written from about the fifth–sixth centuries C.E.

THANKSGIVING—Epistolary section stating cause for thanks to deity—for salvation from danger, or positively, for some blessing. Interchanges with "blessing" in Christian use.